THE LAST PANTHER

THE LAST PANTHER

Slaughter of the Reich

The Breakout from the Halbe Kessel
April-May 1945

WOLFGANG FAUST

Translated from the memoir
'Kesselpanzer'
('Cauldron Panzer')
By Wolfgang Faust

This Edition Published Globally 2016
Bayern Classic Publications

Translated and Edited by Sprech Media

The German terms *'Koenigstiger'* and *'Ritterkreuz'* have been translated as
'King Tiger' and *'Iron Cross'* respectively. While not exact translations,
these are the most widely recognised English terms.
Where appropriate, other German terms are explained in brackets in the text.

ISBN: 1530359708
ISBN-13: 9781530359707

Editor's Introduction

While the apocalyptic struggle for Berlin in 1945 has been extensively discussed by historians, the massive battle of the Halbe Kessel (which took place at the same time) has received less attention. In late April 1945, the entire German Ninth Army was encircled by Red Army forces about 30 km south of Berlin, as the Soviets raced onward to the capital. The Ninth Army, which comprised a mix of Wehrmacht, Waffen SS and ad-hoc units, totalling some 80,000 men, became trapped in a Kessel *('cauldron' or 'pocket')* around a town named Halbe in the Spree Forest. Among them were a large number of civilian refugees, predominantly women and children, fleeing the Soviet advance.

For the German civilians, fear of Soviet occupation was huge: partly a result of Nazi propaganda about 'Red monsters,' but also stemming from knowledge of Red Army crimes against women during the advance. For the troops, there was the fear that capture by the Soviets would lead to deportation to the Soviet Gulag system, in which survival was believed to be only a remote possibility. For both the soldiers and civilians in the Kessel, therefore, escaping and surrendering to the Americans (and not the encircling Soviets) became a desperate priority.

The Ninth Army managed to break out of the Kessel through Halbe, amid scenes of carnage which even veteran troops described as the worst they had witnessed. In a series of splinter groups, fighting vicious but confused battles, the breakout troops and civilians

1

fought through Red Army lines to link up with the German Twelfth Army, who had opened a 'corridor' to them to from the American front in the South West. A few thousand exhausted survivors of the Ninth finally crossed the River Elbe in the closing days of the war, and achieved their goal of surrendering to the Americans; the others were killed or captured by the Soviets.

Among these escapees of the Halbe Kessel was the young Wolfgang Faust, commander of a Panther tank with the 21st Panzer Division, who had spearheaded some of the breakout attempts. After the war, Faust wrote about his combat in the Kessel, in a memoir entitled 'Kesselpanzer,' which remained unpublished in his lifetime. We have now edited and translated 'Kesselpanzer' as 'The Last Panther' for readers in English, and we hope that the horrific human story of the Halbe Kessel will reach a new audience as a result.

As with Faust's only other surviving book ('Tiger Tracks'), this memoir was written with combat still vivid in Faust's mind, and is extremely graphic in its depiction of the final chaotic hours of the Third Reich. Some modern readers may be disturbed by Faust's clinical descriptions of battles, while others will value the remarkable glimpse into the mentality of young German troops who had grown up under the Third Reich. Certainly, 'The Last Panther' gives us insights into a part of the war which has seldom been described by those who were present, and never in such ruthless detail.

While bearing in mind that Faust's world view was rooted in the German mid-twentieth century, and not the sensitivities of the present day, I strongly believe that Faust's two books are a remarkable testament to the catastrophe of 1943-45 for both the Soviets and the Germans. I commend both these memoirs to twenty-first century readers who are seeking to understand the Second World War from *all* its possible perspectives.

Chris Ziedler
May 2015

ENTERING THE KESSEL

In the spring of 1945, the war that we had provoked with such ambition was closing on us like a trap. In January of that year, I was the driver of a Tiger 1 panzer in our defence of the River Oder. In February, my battalion was smashed apart and my commander, Helmann, was burned to death in his turret. By April, in the intense reorganisations required by our collapse, I was made commander of my own panzer with the 21st Panzer Division, part of the great German Ninth Army. My panzer was one of the superb Panthers, the pride of the panzer troops. My rank was now Feldwebel (*sergeant*) and I commanded a crew of teenagers, who looked up to me as if I was a veteran at the age of twenty. Our units tried to hold the Red advance back from Berlin. This was impossible, and we were scattered, while the Reds stormed onward to the capital.

In the last week of April, the trap was shut. The Red forces encircled our entire Ninth Army, South of Berlin, and shut us into a zone of forests where we could only conceal our vehicles and wait for orders.

The hiding was a torment. We sat in our panzers and sweated. Inside the Russian encirclement, inside a pine forest, inside a forty-eight tonne Panther. That was when I realised how completely caught I was; crouched on the commander's chair in the turret, sweat pouring down my back and my heart thumping like a jack hammer. The shadows of Russian bombers were flickering through the pine branches overhead, and the sound of the Russian artillery was loud even through the Panther's armour plate.

We were trapped. Locked in by the Russians, who would ship us to Siberia for sure if they captured us. Our only hope was to reach the American lines on the river Elbe to the West – for the Americans were our great hope now. They were once our enemy, the destroyers of our cities, but they were now our salvation if we could only reach them. To be a prisoner of the 'Amis' meant hot dogs, cabbage and the Geneva Convention. To be a prisoner of the Reds, we were sure, meant slavery, the Arctic Circle and never seeing your homeland again. But there was an entire Russian army between our battle group and the Americans, between our handful of Panthers, our exhausted Panzergrenadiers and a following of civilian refugees who traipsed behind us, sobbing like a funeral procession.

'How long do we have to wait, Herr Feldwebel?' my gunner asked me.

'The Capo will be back soon,' I told him. 'The Capo will know what to do.'

The Capo was our name for our platoon leader, our Leutnant. His original unit of six Panthers was now down to three surviving vehicles, and he was attending an emergency officers' briefing to decide our group's next move.

The air in the Panther turret was foul: monoxide exhaust, shell explosive, oil and five big, hunched young men who hadn't washed for weeks, sweating in the heat. I opened my commander's cupola. Light flooded in through the hatch: clear, spring light scented with pine needles. Through a gap in the trees, I could see white clouds way up in the blue sky. In a second, though, the sky was crossed with vapour trails and the red-starred wings of the Russian planes, and the reek of explosive blew in on the warm breeze.

The sheer hopelessness of our situation came home to me then.

Our three Panthers were parked among the pine trunks in a dense area of forest. To our East, we had a thin screen of troops as a rear guard, but the Russians were probing and testing that line, minute by minute. The sound of their tank engines rose and fell on the breeze, and we could hear the exchanges of fire between our boys and the Russian infantry who rode on the Red panzers. We knew from experience that the Russian commanders didn't like entering forests, whether from tactical reasons or some Slavic superstition, and their huge Josef Stalin panzers, machines as big as Tiger 1 panzers, could not manoeuvre or traverse their gun barrels between the trees unless they knew the pathways that we knew.

To the North West and the South East, two Russian army groups had closed on our location in a pincer of armour and mechanized infantry, crushing the few villages outside the woodland. Heiden had been shelled and burned to the ground, its inhabitants dying in the cellars; at Munchehuf, the few remaining civilian women had been raped for hours in the village square. Our reconnaissance men had watched this from the forest, their hearts torn between taking sniper's shots at the rapists and keeping their location hidden. Schlepzig, a village of dairies and water mills, was blown to pieces by incendiary Katyusha rocket fire, the ditch where its last families took refuge becoming their tomb. Now a solid ring of Russian forces stood around us.

Here in the forest, where we were hiding like wounded animals, our three Panther panzers and several King Tiger panzers of the Waffen SS Panzer Corps were isolated with a group of some five thousand men. Wehrmacht Volksgrenadiers, Waffen SS elite troops, a company of Fallschirmjager (*paratroopers*), and huge numbers of the inevitable stragglers: more Wehrmacht men, Panzer troops who had lost their vehicles, rear echelon orderlies, Luftwaffe mechanics, artillery men with no guns, and a dozen other types and classes.

Among them, in huddles and bunches throughout the trees were groups of civilians. These were women, children and elderly men who had fled their homes in the farms and hamlets as the Reds advanced. With their possessions of a lifetime reduced to bundles, or piles of things in hand carts, they sat in the shadows, staring at the sky above the treetops, or walking up and down like caged creatures in their allotted spaces between the trees and the soldiers.

Among them, I saw our Capo returning from his briefing, his mottled camouflage uniform well suited to the dappled light, his face fixed in his permanent frown of concentration, his Iron Cross worn proudly at his throat. He walked past the knots of civilians without glancing at them. Only when an aircraft passed very low over the tree canopy, low enough to send pine cones down among us like toy hand grenades, only then did he look up at the sky.

We all looked up.

From the tops of the pine trees, small pieces of paper were emerging, floating down and twisting in the breeze. Most became stuck among the branches, but a few slipped between and span slowly down to the forest floor. I grabbed one as it fluttered across the turret, and looked at it. It was a leaflet in neat, printed German:

Reich Forces!
Your position is surrounded by our armies, and the end
of the war is imminent. Do not waste more lives. Any soldier bringing this leaflet to the Russian lines will be treated
well, and all civilians will be given food and shelter.
We all know that the war is almost over.
Why fight on for no purpose? Save yourselves!
After nightfall your safety cannot be guaranteed

The leaflet was grabbed from my hand by the Capo, who scanned it, crouching on the Panther's engine deck, and then laughed.

'Ah, so we'll be treated well!' he chuckled, slapping me on the back. 'What do you think, Faust? Shall we risk it?'

I mimed indecision, stroking my chin.

'It sounds a very generous offer, sir.'

'I hear those hotels in Siberia are very spacious,' he laughed grimly, as he gestured to the other tank crews to come over and join us. 'And there's as much snow as you can eat every day.'

'I don't know, Herr Leutnant,' I said. 'Russian snow doesn't agree with me.'

'Nor me, Faust.' The Capo winked and put the leaflet in his pocket. 'I'll use this paper later, by myself, over a hole in the ground.'

Some of the civilians, though, had grabbed the leaflets and were studying them, debating the proposition in urgent voices. The Capo turned his back on them and gathered the three of our Panther crews, fifteen men in all, at the rear of our Panther, where the big exhaust tubes stood at head height.

'Very well,' the Capo said, surveying his men. 'We're caught like rats in a sack here.'

The men nodded, knowing this was the truth.

'And there's one thing in that *verdamm* leaflet which is true,' the Capo went on. 'The war is coming to a close. We have to accept that fact, if we haven't already. After the war, Germany will still exist, and Germany will need men like us to rebuild, to make it strong again and to look after the people. Germany will need us as much in the next few years as it has in the past six years, I can tell you that. But for us to serve Germany in the future, we must surrender to the Americans. That is our task now.'

We panzer crews glanced at each other. The war coming to an end? Germany to be occupied, and then rebuilt? These were massive ideas, and difficult to accept – but the Capo kept us focussed on more immediate concerns.

'In this part of the forest, we are just one of many encircled groups of the Ninth Army. All these groups must move West, and assemble in the Spree Forest. We will do so at first light. From the Spree, we will put our panzer forces together, and break out to the West in one coordinated movement, spearheaded by our heaviest available armour. At the same time, the Twelfth Army will fight their way up from the River Elbe to meet us, and they will form a corridor through which our forces can move to the West and the Americans.'

The crews reacted instinctively, giving the Capo a series of tactical questions.

Who would lead the final breakout from the Spree Forest?

The King Tiger panzers of the SS Panzer Corps. They would be the sledgehammer, breaking the path open through the Red lines.

Who would be the rear guard when we broke out of the Spree Forest?

The remnants of the 32nd Panzer Division. They would hold off the Reds from the east while the escape corridor was opened.

Supplies of ammunition?

No more was available. Each Panther had thirty rounds remaining, half its standard amount.

Fuel?

There was no fuel available. Gasoline would have to be found from abandoned vehicles or supplies on the route West.

The men nodded grimly. We all noticed that the Capo, usually so precise, had not produced a map or diagram of the planned route or the enemy positions. That meant he had no map. Well, so be it.

'Herr Leutnant, what of the civilians?'

The Capo hesitated for a moment – again, this was unlike him. 'The civilians? If they can keep up and follow us, let them,' he said quietly. 'Otherwise, they will have to remain here.'

'All of them?'

'Yes, all of them. They must struggle on alone. We cannot evacuate them and we cannot help them. If we stay here, both the civilians and the troops are lost. If we break out, at least some troops will be saved for the future of our country.'

'But, Herr Leutnant, the women,' one of the Panther commanders said. 'To leave them to the Reds, to be raped, killed?'

The Capo took a long breath and fixed his eyes on the armour plate of the Panther beside him.

'We cannot help them,' he repeated. 'This is a national tragedy. We are seeking to seize some good from this disaster, from the events that have happened. This is our duty now.'

'But, Herr Leutnant – '

'This is our duty. We will move at first light.'

In the spring dusk, the sound of fighting from the East was very clear. It was clear, also, to the civilians camped among us, the young mothers with children who sat pale and hunched over improvised stoves, while their kids scrabbled among the pine needles and earth. It was clear to the old men who stood staring at the stoves, sucking on pieces of stale bread from their haversacks. These civilians asked us no questions – they could tell by the way we were preparing the panzers, checking the engines over and sharing out the ammunition between the crews – they could tell that we were moving out. Up to now, we had moved slowly where possible, enabling the civilians to walk after us with their carts and bundles. Now we would be charging, making a wild dash for the Spree Forest with the other battered remnants of the Ninth Army, with no time to wait for the non-combatants.

To reconnoitre the immediate route ahead for this breakout at dawn, I went forward with the Capo on foot. We left the encampment and walked, with our MP40s in our hands, through a series of paths between the trees, remembering the route from previous scouting forays. The pines thinned, and we came within sight of the edge of the forest, where the trees gave way to a sandy plain dotted at intervals with craters, lakes and areas of marsh.

That was the way to the Spree Forest and the West.

It was an unpromising piece of terrain to advance across: open and soft, full of features which could bog a panzer down or leave it stranded to the Red fire. The plain was strewn in places with wrecked vehicles, trucks, cars and Hanomag half-tracks which had attempted to cross it two days previously as the Russian pincers were closing on our forest hiding places.

The Capo and I went on foot further than we had been before, along the edge of the trees, where abandoned equipment, weapons and supplies showed where the final troops had tried to flee before the trap closed.

There were many corpses along this way, too. Many were Wehrmacht troops, hit by shellfire or by incendiaries that left the trees smouldering. The smell of ash, pine sap and human decay hung thick in the air here, untouched by the warm breeze. There were bodies, too, of civilians who had tried to dash across after the troops. One group of women had been pushing a handcart, and their shattered bodies lay among the pine cones, staring up at the branches. The quilts and bowls from their cart lay around them. After that –

'My God,' said the Capo. 'What has happened here?'

A small battle had taken place on the edge of the woodland, where a rough track led out into the plain. A section of German infantry were lying dead in the burned-out shell of their truck. Behind them, another group of women lay dead – but these women had been stripped, their naked bodies bearing witness to the violation they had endured in their final moments. Each had a bullet hole in her forehead – five bodies in all, five shots to the forehead.

'This is what awaits our civilians,' the Capo muttered. 'And yet we can't bring them with us.'

We ducked into the shadows as a pair of Soviet fighters raced over the treeline. The planes strafed the open plain for no evident reason, their cannon fire ripping through the abandoned vehicles there, setting some alight in spouts of flame. Then there was the echo of their departure, and the constant noise of the fighting beyond the forest.

The Capo turned away from the women's bodies, and pointed out across the plain.

'The SS King Tigers will go first,' he said. 'They will move at speed, close to the forest where the ground is firmer. We will follow them, and hold off any Reds that appear on the flanks of the plain. The infantry will move behind us on the edges of the trees. Then we will charge down the slope towards the village of Markhof, and go through it. The main Ninth Army is assembling five kilometres beyond there, in the Spree forest beyond the plain. When we are with them, then the fighting will really start.'

I nodded, looking at the path along the edge of the trees. We would be moving like ducks on a fairground shooting stall, one after the other. Even now, there were surely Russian eyes in Markhof, on the other side of the plain, or hidden among the trees in the forests on either side, watching our trees for signs of a breakout. The Russians had limitless ammunition, endless supplies of their panzers, infinite quantities of troops which they regarded as expendable. All that, against our few King Tigers and three Panthers, and a rag-tag army of hungry and disoriented infantry desperate to reach the Americans. So desperate that they would abandon their own civilians to the Reds.

There was no other way.

Dusk was gathering, and, as we went back to the encampment, the horizon beyond the plain was illuminated by tall columns of flame, stretching to a great height under the stars. We guessed these were the remains of one of our transport columns that had been caught on the other side of the open ground. How many trucks, panzers and wagons would have to burn to create such a pillar of fire? Closer at hand, the sky was lit by flares as the Russians tried to illuminate the forest. One parachute flare drifted down on top of us, its white magnesium setting the pine branches alight and turning the whole area to daylight until we scrambled away from its glare, back into our hiding place deep in the trees.

Although no lights or fires were visible, it seemed that the whole forest was awake in the twilight, and working like devils. We passed shadowy areas where we knew the Waffen SS King Tiger panzers were concealed under piles of branches, and we heard sounds of these branches being thrown aside and the mighty engines trial-started. In other areas, our infantry were readying themselves for the first light. Nobody was sleeping – how could they, knowing what the morning would bring? Among them, the cries of civilian children, and their mothers, reminded us of the imminent fate of these compatriots as soon as the Reds moved into the forest. I put that out of my mind, and went back to my Panther.

My crew were good soldiers: in the last daylight, they were cleaning out the Panther's long gun barrel, using the six-metre long rods to drag a wad of cloth down the barrel, using a new wad each time until the cloth passed down the tube clean. This scoured the rifled bore clean of explosive residue, ensuring the gun would fire accurately and without warping. We also checked over the tracks, the lubrication points inside the turret, the hydraulics and the oil filters above the engine. Then we sat inside the Panther: myself, my gunner and our loader on our perches in the turret; the radio man at his machine gun point in the hull, and the driver beside him at the controls.

Were we sleeping? Or were we awake and thinking of the morning's battle to come? I did both, moving between sleep and thought, as flashes and explosions lit up the glass of my cupola periscopes.

———

At first light, the civilians stood to watch us go. Grey, spectral figures in their shawls and blankets, the children clinging to the women's knees, some began to form up behind us as we started our engines. The Panthers' exhausts sent up sparks into the air, lighting the civilians in flickering red and orange. I had my last sight of them from the cupola: a phalanx of these forms, stumbling and running after us as the Panthers swayed between the trees towards the plain.

Then the infantry came out to follow us.

In a few seconds, huge groups of our infantry emerged behind us from every shadow and gap in the trees, swarming in the dust and fumes we threw out, knocking aside the few women who could still keep up, and finally blotting out the last of the civilians behind a solid wall of ragged, grey and blue uniforms. In the dawn light, they were unshaven, haggard, their eyes filled with blank determination. The civilians, left in their wake, were on their own now. The dash to the Spree Forest was beginning.

My Panther turret was humid, filled with fumes and the roar of the Maybach engine through the crew compartment wall. We moved at walking pace between the trees, following an old forestry track lined with the hulks of abandoned vehicles, felled trees, wounded men unable to walk who looked hopelessly for help, and at every moment more and more of our infantry were emerging from the depths of the forest, ready to join the escape route to the West. As we neared the edge of the trees, close to where I had patrolled with the Capo in the dusk, we came on a phenomenal sight.

Two of our massive King Tiger panzers were already in position to make the first bid to leave the forest. Almost one and a half times the weight of my Panther, they towered over the narrow path, belching exhaust fumes, their mottled camouflage well adapted to the light and shade conditions. Their ultra-long 88mm gun barrels projected to the West, away from the density of trees – with such a long barrel, the danger was that it would hit the trees as the vehicle manoeuvred. The commanders were visible in the turret cupolas, their faces blank, betraying no emotion at all. As they saw us, they waited barely a few seconds more, and then the Tigers shook and moved towards the plain. The air behind them quivered with the heat of their exhaust, and their tracks threw out branches and clods of earth as the massive steel treads bit the earth.

On the edge of the forest, a squad of engineers were at work cutting down a handful of remaining trees with axes: the final trees that screened the interior of the woods and prevented vehicles exiting or entering. One by one the trees toppled, and as the last one fell, the two Tigers crushed it under their tracks as they advanced over the debris. Smashing aside the carcasses of burned-out trucks, the two Tigers moved out to the edge of the plain. Behind them, another King Tiger emerged from the depths between the trees, its sloping front plate and long, slim turret draped with foliage. It misjudged the narrow passage between the trees, and had to ram down a series of huge pines to reach the perimeter, wasting time and petrol and risking a damaged track in the process of destroying the trunks. Finally, in a hurricane of fumes, sparks, crashing trees and roaring engines, the King Tigers were out on the plain and advancing along the treeline towards the West.

The Russians responded immediately.

As our Panther manoeuvred up to the exit point, past the massed lines of infantry being held back by their officers, I put my forehead to the periscope and squinted along the treeline. I could see the last of the King Tigers ahead of us, blowing sparks in the grey light, with its turret pointing left across the plain to the opposing side. In seconds, a flash of tracer struck it on the side of the turret, and a shell deflected off the angled side wall and span off into the trees, still glowing brightly. The Tiger rocked, but kept moving, traversing its gun to aim at the possible origin of the shot. I ordered my gunner, who had control of the turret traverse through his foot pedals, to rotate our gun likewise. Through the aiming bracket on my cupola, I saw only a solid wall of shadowy trees, with mist hanging between them, betraying no sign of enemy activity. Then the tracer came again, and flashed across the plain towards the King Tiger.

I saw the shell hit the Tiger, on the rear this time, near the tracks and the idler wheel at the back. This was a high explosive round, and it burst in a white star. I saw the entire rear wheel of the Tiger – a metal disc that took three men to lift it – fly off and tumble away over the grassland. The Tiger's track links fragmented and span out, and the whole seventy-tonne panzer slewed around out of control to one side, blocking the way ahead in a spray of earth and stones as it came to a halt, its track hanging out behind it, quivering with the beat of the panzer's engine. Those Red gunners knew how to bring down a King Tiger in stages: not with armour-piercing rounds, but firstly by blowing the running gear off, leaving it stranded.

I saw the origin of the shot, though, and called it out to my gunner, as he had control of the Panther's turret. In the trees, where the mist was dissipating, above a small lake of reeds...there! There was the outline of a T34 tank, wreathed in the smoke of its gun.

On my order, our driver slowed and halted to give us firing stability. My gunner grunted as the Panther rocked and went still, then he laid the shot with the hydraulic controls, and fired. The tracer streaked out and the Panther bucked gently, as our muzzle brake and hydraulic dampers absorbed the gun's recoil.

We moved again, and approached the stranded King Tiger. Over in the trees, I saw that our shell had hit the T34, because its frontal plate was emitting a dark smoke, and it was beginning to advance out of the tree line to shorten the range against us. Ahead, the damaged Tiger was firing at the T34, its hull rocking as it discharged the shot. It fired again, and then again, and I realised that the crew were determined to fire all their ammunition before they relinquished the stricken vehicle. From the opposing treeline, I saw through my periscopes more T34s emerging from the woods, knocking trees aside as they lumbered out to face us. For panzers which were barely equal in armour and weaponry to the Panther, let alone the King Tiger, they showed no hesitation in streaming out towards our panzers, slewing around the ridges and ponds in the plain.

The King Tiger in front of us fired like the devil himself, sending round after round screaming onto the row of six T34s that advanced on us. The Tiger's massive 88mm gun made short work of two of the Red panzers immediately. One Red was struck on the turret, smashing off a large scab of metal plate which shot away across the plain in a stream of sparks. The T34 whirled around, out of control, and crashed nose-down in a bed of reeds. I told my gunner not to fire on it, but to conserve ammunition, as it was already starting to burn. The Tiger hit the second T34 directly through the glacis plate, and I saw large pieces of the hull fly off as the Red machine exploded inside.

My own gunner hit a third Red tank as it raced towards us, hitting it in the gun mantle with a force that knocked the top surface of the Red's turret completely away from the walls. The T34 kept advancing on us, with its dead commander hanging out of the broken turret, his body on fire. We did not fire on it, but let it approach, slowly running out of momentum, until it stopped and erupted in an orange fireball.

I checked all round in the periscopes to assess the situation now. The remaining three T34s were retreating in reverse gear, keeping their thick front plates facing us, firing wildly with their undoubtedly ample supply of ammunition. The King Tiger was shooting at them, clearly determined to get a strike with its last rounds. It shot one of the retreating Red tanks through the front track, which unwound and shed itself loose. That T34 veered to one side, crashed down into a depression, and tipped over, with its upper hull exposed and its working track still running freely. The Tiger fired one last shot, and pierced the tank through the engine deck. The whole vehicle shook as the engine exploded, and even as the Red crew men struggled to leap from the hatches, its fuel erupted in a furnace that lit the heath for a wide radius. I looked away as the burning crew men disappeared in the flames, to see the King Tiger crew disembarking and gesturing to my Panther for assistance.

In the forests beside the King Tiger, massed ranks of our infantry were moving between the trees, rushing onward after the leading King Tigers which were rolling ahead towards the West. Behind us, the Capo's Panther and our third Panther brought up the rear, as we had planned, shielding the infantry from further attacks.

I allowed the stranded King Tiger crew to climb onto our Panther, and in moments they were clinging onto the back deck among the engine fumes. As we skirted around their abandoned vehicle, I saw it explode internally, the hatches blowing out and tumbling into the air. The crew, professional to the last, had set a demolition charge to prevent the powerful machine being captured by the Reds. After that, we were rolling ahead again, keeping on our right the forest with its moving mass of men, and the plain on our left. About six hundred metres ahead, the King Tigers were leading the way, their great turrets rising and falling as the hulls ploughed across the undulating ground. We had progressed about two kilometres, and had three more kilometres to go until we reached the village. The light was increasing, and the pines began to show their green hue as the day began to break.

I wiped the sweat from my face. Could it be that we were going to succeed, to break through? The Red forces seemed unresponsive, other than that brief counter attack from the unit of T34s. But I knew the Reds too well to assume that they were sleeping or distracted. At every moment, with every creak of the Panther's running gear, every growl of the Maybach engine, I expected more trouble.

It came in the form of a massive bombardment, a hail of rockets which appeared from over the tree canopy to the west, trailing plumes of sparks, and shot down onto our column in fractions of a second.

'Katyushas,' I shouted. 'Keep us moving, driver, in the name of God.'

The rockets smashed into the ground along the treeline, bursting between my panzer and the King Tiger up ahead, and showering us with shrapnel which smacked off our armour plate with hollow impacts. I looked to the rear through the periscope, and glimpsed the Tiger crew on our engine deck sheltering behind our turret. A Katyusha exploded behind us, and two of those crew men were blown off our hull, falling into the path of the Capo's Panther behind us. I saw that Panther swerve, but I could not see if he avoided crushing the men. In the trees beside us, the rockets were exploding in whirlwinds of destruction, felling tall trunks and sending them flailing around. Underneath them, the massed lines of infantry were running like men possessed, leaping over the wounded and dying as they fought to get ahead, to get out of this fire zone.

The rockets changed then from high explosive to incendiary, and they exploded among the trees in sheets of liquid flame which cascaded down onto the fleeing men below, covering the unlucky ones in a torrent of fire. Men ran on fire, jumped and rolled with their uniforms and rifles burning on their backs. Other men jumped over them, ducking between the pouring flames in their frantic search for a way through.

Ahead, I saw two King Tigers outlined against the exploding flames, at a point where the forest wall fell away and the plain sloped downward towards the village of Markhof, which we would have to traverse. I saw the huge vehicles slow, with dust shooting up from their tracks, and then come to a halt on the plain, away from the burning trees. Why had they stopped there, on the crest of the ridge itself, on the top of the slope where they could be readily seen? With the Katyushas still bursting around us, we approached the King Tigers, and then came level with them, our Panther tipping over the crest of the ridge beside them, to face downwards.

I could see immediately why even a King Tiger would halt when faced with that slope.

The village of Markhof itself was clearly visible, with flames rising from its outlying houses, its slender church spire pointing up through the smoke. The slope leading from us to the settlement rolled down at a gradual gradient for about two kilometres, the scrubland steaming with dew in the early warmth. This slope was absolutely alive with explosions.

It was being bombarded with heavy artillery from the Red sectors, with shells big enough to scoop up chunks of earth the size of automobiles and throw them high into the air, disintegrating as they fell. The slope was strewn with abandoned and burned-out vehicles, the flotsam of our final elements who reached the West before the encirclement. As I watched, an abandoned eight-wheel armoured car was hit by a shell and thrown to the height of a house into the air, its tyres spinning off in all directions. For any vehicle to cross this zone of death was an invitation to destruction.

The Capo contacted me on the radio set, my wireless man connecting me through the headset.

'We will have to go ahead,' he shouted. 'We cannot stop. See, the Tigers are moving now.'

Yes – the two great King Tigers were beginning their charge down the slope, their angled front plates set squarely in the direction of the village down there, with their long gun barrels pointing at the houses.

'If we can take the village and the road through it,' the Capo shouted. 'The infantry can get through. Follow the Tigers.'

'My God,' our gunner said suddenly. 'My God, Herr Feldwebel – there are wounded down there.'

As we began to move onto the gradient, into the whirlwind of explosions, with shrapnel smashing into our armour plate, I saw that the gunner was correct. To one side of the slope, a series of trailers on rubber tyres were abandoned, some still hooked to trucks, others simply dumped in the open. These were metal box trailers of a type often used as ambulances, and from their open rear doors I could distinctly see wounded men arranged on tiers inside, some gesturing to us weakly. There were five of these trailers, with perhaps fifty or sixty wounded men in total.

We approached one of these, accelerating and unable to halt or give assistance to the wounded. Our only hope of getting through was to keep moving and minimise our time in the open. As we passed the first trailer, it was rocked by a high-explosive shell which ripped the sides off, and threw the wounded men still on their stretchers across the ground. There was no chance to swerve: our Panther rolled over them without even a bump, crushing their stricken bodies where they lay. Our driver groaned and cursed as this happened, but there was no way to avoid the massacre. The other trailers that we passed were filled with the terrified faces of wounded men, huddling together as the shells exploded around them, knowing that death could strike at any moment. Then we were past these doomed men, and went charging down the slope, rearing and bouncing between the shell bursts, towards the village.

In front of us, I saw the two King Tigers moving like steamrollers down the incline, crushing flat the few vehicles that lay in their paths. One Tiger completely crushed an empty staff car, and the gasoline left in it exploded in a puff of flames under the Tiger's treads. The other Tiger dipped down into a reed bed, and came up streaming with mud and water, its momentum such that even the marshy ground could not hold it back. That Tiger was hit by a shell which exploded on its flank, and its armoured track guards were blown away in a star burst of fire, but the panzer did not slow for a second.

As we raced behind the King Tigers, I checked around for our other two Panthers. The Capo, distinguished by his commander's extended radio aerial, was next to us, but our third Panther was lagging behind, travelling more slowly. It had an engine problem, perhaps, or had taken a shell strike on the running gear. It slowed yet further, falling behind, and I had to turn my attention to the front again.

We were approaching the village, and now we could see Russian PAK *(anti-tank)* guns emplaced in earth embankments around the meadows at the edge. A PAK shell hit us on the front plate with a crash that jarred my teeth, and then another smashed into our turret close to my head, feeling like a blow to the temple. We rolled on, though, and I saw repeated PAK rounds deflecting off the colossal armour of the Tigers in front, tracer rounds spiralling off the hull and turret as the panzers raced through the tornados of shrapnel. One King Tiger was hit by high explosive, but the round burst against the turret and did not damage the tracks.

All of our panzers were swaying, rising and falling now as we lurched over the uneven ground – and this wild movement made it harder, of course, for the Red gunners to target any specific place on our structures. We were travelling at thirty kilometres per hour, bucking and swerving almost out of control, and in a few seconds the enemy PAK emplacements loomed up directly in front of us.

There was no time to slow down - and no need to do so. The King Tigers crashed into the emplacements first, smashing the earth walls aside in a cloud of debris. I saw an entire Red PAK crew turn and flee, but first their gun was chewed to pieces by the

Tiger's tracks, and then the men themselves were scythed down – first by machine gun fire from the panzer, and the survivors by being trampled under the churning tracks themselves. I saw the Tiger's track-work run bright red with flesh, and then we ourselves were colliding with a PAK position, and wreaking the same destruction.

The entire barrel and wheels of a PAK gun rose up in front of us as we broke open its emplacement, the gun revolving in the air as it was thrown to one side by the momentum of our tonnage. The Red gunners, too, were smashed apart, with boots and helmets spinning around our turret as our driver slewed the machine to one side to hit another emplacement. This one caused us to rear up into the air, and I believe we were airborne for a short while – and then our entire weight came hurtling down on the gun underneath us. I heard and felt the Red ammunition detonate under us, but by then we were beyond the emplacement and careering towards the houses of the village.

I could see Red troops running from us through the one main street, and others firing on us with small arms or hurling grenades. I opted to use some precious ammunition, and ordered my gunner to clear the settlement. Two rounds of our high explosive sent the remaining Reds scrambling away, and the firing against us ground to a halt.

We came to rest with a mighty thump, up against the earth wall of a farmer's animal enclosure, where many dead cattle lay with their legs stiffened upward. To our right, the two King Tigers were firing intermittently into the village, and beside me the Capo's Panther advanced into the main street, firing down it towards the square that we could see at the far end.

I looked back at the slope behind us. Our third comrade Panther was stranded on the incline, with black smoke drifting from its engine. It was shuddering and making jerking movements as it tried to advance, but the running gear was evidently seized. Behind it, a mass of German infantry were already surging, not in disciplined ranks but in a mob of field-grey, blue and camouflage uniforms, running each man for himself down the slope towards us, through the smoke of the bombardment still swirling in the air. The sun was rising behind them in the East, and this lit the smouldering trees of the pine forest in a lurid glow, showing up the folds of the ground and the debris the men were scrambling over.

This frantic horde managed to cover a hundred metres or so, before the Katyusha rockets came down on them again. In the time we had charged down the hill, the Soviet rocket gunners had clearly recalibrated their launchers onto the slope – and now the high-explosive and incendiary warheads came screaming in again, directly into the mass of charging infantry.

The stranded Panther was hit first, even as the horde of infantry swarmed past it. With a colossal impact, the turret of the panzer was blown completely off the hull, flinging the panzer crew out into the charging mass of infantry, where they disappeared under the hundreds of boots. A second shell exploded among the running figures, and then another – until I turned my eyes away from the carnage and the whirling, fragmented bodies.

In front of us, I could make out through the dusty periscope glass the pasture before the village, the shattered houses and the rear plate of the Capo's Panther as he traversed his turret left and right in the middle of the main street, probing for resistance. I saw a group of Red soldiers slip out of a doorway on his right, clutching small packages which could only be anti-panzer mines. My gunner saw them too, and fired a burst of MG from the co-axial gun. The Reds sprawled on the cobbles, their bodies rolling over as the bullets propelled them across the stones. On my left, the two massive King Tigers rumbled up into the edges of the village, standing against the picturesque, timbered buildings in stark outline. They progressed slowly around the edge of the settlement, using an unsurfaced road that ran beside the village through its water meadows.

Even as my Panther began to enter the village, the German infantry were on our heels. Hundreds of our ragged, emaciated comrades began to pour off the slopes and run, walk or hobble after the King Tigers, while some – those best-armed and seemingly most alert – cautiously came in behind us to the village centre, fanning out along the frontages and sweeping the gardens for concealed enemy troops.

In the main square, as the Capo's Panther and mine halted with our eyes on a row of Russian trucks that could be exploited for fuel, a handful of Red prisoners were dragged together – men who had been hiding in cellars or gardens, disarmed and reluctant to fight. We set them to work immediately, once we had ascertained that the trucks used gasoline and not diesel. The prisoners were put to work, using our hand pumps to siphon off the precious fuel from their trucks and transfer it to the two surviving Panthers.

Several shells fell among the houses, blowing the roofs off and causing gable walls to collapse, but the bombardment seemed to be slackening in intensity – the Russian artillery perhaps not realising that their men were no longer in control of the village. In this comparative lull, many German civilians emerged and began to gather around the Panthers, begging us to take them with us, away from the encircling Reds.

'Our way forward is through the Spree Forest to the West,' the Capo said to them. 'That is a dangerous journey, and we cannot slow down for you.'

'Come inside here and see something,' one old man said to us. 'Come.'

While the Red prisoners were still pumping the fuel, the old man took the Capo and myself into the largest building on the square – an ancient council chamber surmounted by an ornate weather vane. It took time for my eyes to adjust to the dim light inside, which was filtered through coloured glass windows. In this old council hall, on the wood floorboards polished by generations of villagers' feet, there was a row of young women, naked on the floor. Their bodies glowed a waxy colour in the faint light, among the wounds and splashes of blood that covered their bodies. From a ceiling beam, two men were hanging from nooses, their necks broken, their open eyes staring down at the corpses of –

'Their daughters,' the man explained. 'They were made to watch this, and then they were hanged.'

Back outside, the Capo allowed the civilians to climb onto the panzers. Then he took his Walther pistol and, when the Red soldiers had finished pumping the fuel, he took them to one side and shot them dead, in the back of the neck, one after the other against the council chamber wall.

A circle of villagers, troops and us panzer crews watched this – and then we moved out of the settlement, towards the woodland beyond where we could see the King Tigers halted under the first trees of the Spree Forest, our objective. A throng of several hundred civilians followed our Panthers on foot into the woods. We went past the King Tigers, and now it was we who led the way. The civilians proved helpful – one woman perched on my turret, with a carbine slung over her shoulder, and pointed out to me the broadest tracks to take to enable us to reach the dense, central part of the forest most quickly.

As we moved out of sight of the village, I heard the scream of aero engines.

A trio of Red aircraft, the type known as the Sturmovik, was racing over the village, strafing with cannon. I saw the remaining red-tiled roofs of the houses fracture in sparks, until, as we rounded a corner in the track and moved finally away, the whole village was enveloped in a whirlwind of smoke and ash.

The Russians had realised that we had broken through. But what happened to Markhof was behind us now, and we had to forget it. We were where we aimed to be, in the Spree Forest itself, and now we had to move across it and break out to the West.

'Well, we are in the Kessel,' the Capo said to me on the radio from his Panther. 'We are Kessel panzers now.'

A Kessel: a cauldron, a boiling pot. A Kessel is a pocket of troops who are surrounded, but won't give up or surrender. A Kessel is a living, breathing stew, of troops and civilians, of panzers, vehicles, horses and carts. We were part of the Kessel now.

—

BREAKOUT FROM THE KESSEL

To say that we were not alone in the Kessel would be a terrible understatement. The Kessel consisted of the entire Spree Forest, East of a small town called Halbe, which was a place that I had never heard of before, but would never be able to forget. The Spree contained ancient oak, pine and birch groves which stretched perhaps thirty kilometres from East to West, punctuated by small lakes, heaths and firebreak channels where no trees grew. This whole area was alive with people – with tens of thousands of people, we began to realise, as we penetrated deeper into the woods, heading West.

The forest tracks – bare earth roads meant for forestry wagons, not an army – were full of people walking, limping, driving and riding to the West. Some were soldiers, of all ranks, insignia and uniforms, including Wehrmacht, Waffen SS and Volkssturm (*civilian defence force*) troops, all mingled together. The Volkssturm men were dressed in civilian clothes, with Panzerfausts (*single-shot bazookas*) and the crude sub machine guns manufactured specifically for their use. Some of the troops were wounded, and they walked on crutches or they travelled by climbing onto any vehicle that would accept them – whether a panzer, truck or horse cart. Men slept on the decks of panzers crawling slowly along the roads, or sat on the turrets, on the track covers or the gun barrels themselves, their heads swaying as they slept upright.

Many were civilians – elderly men, women of all ages, and large numbers of children, all mixed with the troops, riding or begging for places alongside the soldiers. Some of the civilians were armed with shotguns, pistols or military carbines, and walked almost like troops, with only backpacks and their guns. Others were trying to move their possessions in handcarts or wagons pulled by horses or oxen. Some refugees had brought their animals with them, and it was not unusual for our Panther crew men to jump down and clear a path through a huddle of cows, pigs or goats being driven by an old farmer with a stick.

Behind our two surviving Panthers, the SS King Tigers gave lifts to SS men only –dozens of men on each panzer, their camouflage uniforms blending in well against the foliage and dappled light.

On this narrow track, full of obstructions and abandoned vehicles, our progress was agonisingly slow, and we saw terrible sights as we passed through between the oak trees. Several times, Soviet aircraft flew over the tree canopy, firing randomly down at the forest floor, evidently not caring whether they hit anything, or what it was that they shot up. One such strafing attack sent a volley of cannon tracer tearing diagonally through the branches, ripping off heavy boughs and setting them alight. One tree limb crashed down onto a family pushing a handcart – a mother, grandmother and children – killing the two women. Their bodies were left in the undergrowth, and the dazed children took a few possessions from their cart, and simply started walking again, with no protection at all, soon disappearing in the column of foot traffic. Katyusha rockets also exploded in the trees, the shrapnel raining down on us along with splinters of wood that tore into the people clinging to the vehicles.

The civilian woman acting as my guide, who was standing on my rear deck, was hit in the arm by such a splinter, and I gave her a bandage from our field dressing pack. She bandaged herself with gritted teeth, her eyes full of tears.

At one point, in the afternoon, we halted to add oil to the engines and allow them to cool, as the crawling progress was overheating them dangerously. We steered our two Panthers off the track, and bulldozed aside several young trees to form a space away from the road without causing a break in the overhead foliage. As the Panther's engine shut down, the metal clanged while it contracted, and the great Maybach unit hissed to itself in the shade. The King Tigers pulled up next to us, their engine decks emitting a haze of oily smoke, and their crewmen opened up the engine grilles to allow cooling.

The Panther and Tiger engines were of a similar design: a motor unit encased in a solid armoured steel box, with the radiators in separate steel boxes on either side. This was intended to give protection from water if the panzer had to ford a river, because few bridges could take the forty-eight tonne weight of the Panther or the almost seventy tonnes of the King Tiger. But this protective design caused the motor unit to overheat easily in its steel coffin, and engine fires were a common problem.

We poured in the last of our oil, then told our accompanying infantry that we would stop for one hour. We took the chance to check our track links and running gear while the infantry sprawled on the forest floor among the leaves and scrub. On the edge of our temporary clearing, some of the men were investigating a parked car: a German Horsch staff car, of the kind used by senior officers. They called us over to see what they had found.

In the driver's seat, an SS officer was sitting, staring through the wind shield, his head slumped against the door. He had shot himself through the temple, very recently – the pistol was in his hand, and the blood dripping from his head was still wet. Beside him, a woman in civilian clothes – an elegant summer dress and hat – was also dead, her hands clasped demurely in her lap, her eyes shut and a cigarette between her lips.

The SS were in terror of the Reds now. After the years of laying waste to Russia, the pits full of bodies, the policy of taking no prisoners, the SS knew that the Reds would show them no mercy. And why should the Reds show mercy, after all? The SS had done things during their three years inside Russia which could barely be expressed in words. It was far better for an SS man to die with a bullet through his head, and with his pretty mistress beside him, than fall into the hands of the vengeful Soviets.

There was nothing to be done about these two bodies in the Horsch car. We siphoned off their petrol tank, which was almost full, and shared it out among the panzers.

The shadows were lengthening when we moved off again. The forest held so much life, so much death, and every angle in the track revealed new confusion and suffering. Civilians on foot called out to us endlessly, asking which way they should go, pleading for the chance to ride on the panzers. Some held their children out to us, showing us how exhausted and ill they were, telling us how far they had trekked on foot – for one hundred, or two hundred kilometres from the East. We could do nothing for these people, and at times our gunner had to use a shovel to beat back civilian men who tried to climb onto our hull.

As the evening came on, my civilian guide told me that there were three or four kilometres remaining before we reached the central area of the forest.

'We will have to be careful there,' she added.

'We?' I asked her.

'I assume I can remain with your panzer,' she said. 'As I have been helpful to your unit.'

'How is your arm?'

'Painful.'

'I wish I had morphine to give you.'

'You have none in your medical bag? My arm is very painful now. Why don't you give me morphine, Herr Feldwebel?'

'We have used it all, madam.'

'I do not believe you,' she hissed, clutching her arm. 'I think you are saving it for yourselves.'

I said nothing, but as the Panther rumbled to yet another halt, at a junction of three roadways clogged with carts and even a civilian bus, crammed with wounded, I looked at her carefully for the first time. She was perhaps forty years of age, with grey eyes that were burning with indignation.

'Just a little morphine,' she repeated. 'Please.'

In front of our Panther, an ambulance cart was stuck, its horse collapsing on its forelegs in exhaustion, the wounded troops in the wagon crying out as they were jolted by the people swarming past.

'I used the last of my panzer crew's morphine two days ago,' I said. 'One of my men was hit by a shell splinter. In the kidneys. It took him three days to die, but we kept him out of pain for as long as we could. When our morphine ran out, he begged me to shoot him.'

She wiped her nose with her hand, evidently chastened.

'And did you shoot him?'

'Yes, I shot him in the head. I hope someone does that to me if I'm in that condition. But listen, I'll find you some morphine along the road here somewhere. You have been useful.'

The sounds of battle were loud to the south and east, and it seemed that even in the Kessel the Russians were probing at our forces and wearing us down. Infantrymen ran in from the perimeters, shouting that the Reds were forcing their way into the Kessel in groups of two or three panzers.

The trees began to thin slightly, and at intervals it was possible to see the outlines of Soviet aircraft moving over the tree canopy in the blue evening sky. We tore down more foliage to drape over our hulls and turrets, and watched the sky with a desperate urgency before we moved along any stretch of the track that was even slightly exposed.

At an exposed clearing among the trees, we encountered a unit of three Jagdpanzers – low tank destroyers on a Panzer IV chassis, an excellent weapon – and we halted behind them while they scanned the open gap in the treetops for planes. The first Jagdpanzer moved away, surging along the exposed track and beyond it into deeper, thicker forest. The second vehicle paused, revved and did likewise, dashing through the clearing. The final Jagdpanzer took a long time to check the sky – until our troops were calling out to it to move or get off of the path. Its commander ignored the cries, if he could even hear them, and finally gave the command to move.

Just as the low, squat vehicle lurched off onto the clearing, the shapes of Sturmoviks tore over us, their shadows filling the roadway. The Jagdpanzer accelerated, committed now to making a break for the denser trees, and made it half way. Then a volley of rockets smashed down through the trees, splitting the branches apart, and struck the Jagdpanzer directly on its flank.

The machine reared up into the air, crashed down on its tracks and lost control. With smoke pouring from its grilles, it veered sideways into the trees beside the road, knocking down several in its momentum and tipping over onto its side. The trees swayed and crashed to the ground – and this only exposed the stretch of road more brutally, giving the Red pilots a clearer view of what was down there in the forest. Flames poured from the Jagdpanzer's engine as it came to a stop in a whirl of broken wood, its upper deck facing the break in the tree cover.

The people clinging to my Panther leaped off and began running into the deeper forest, as everybody could see what was about to happen. Civilians, troops and medics – all leaped and scrambled away from us, away from the target of the Sturmoviks. Only the civilian woman stayed, clinging to the turret rear, apparently too fearful to move, as I scanned the sky for returning aircraft. I saw none and could hear none – and told my driver to drive like a devil across the clearing. It was a risk – but it was riskier to stay where we were, with the tree cover broken and the Jagdpanzer on fire to mark the target.

I dropped down into the turret, and my driver put us in motion with a force that flung me back against the rear wall. Through the periscopes, I saw the trees flashing past, and the burning panzer, with a crewman trying to drag himself out of the hatch, his whole torso on fire. Then the road in front of us lit up with exploding rockets, which ripped up the earth and trees, and sent a barrage of shrapnel over the panzer, the fragments hammering on the hull as we swept over the smoke of the explosion.

The panzers behind us did not delay in making their move, and in a minute, both our Panthers and the two King Tigers were across and moving into the comparative safety of the thicker tree cover. After some distance, we paused, and I went up through the cupola to assess the state of the hull. Around us, our troops and civilians were slowly reassembling, having run after us through the trees.

On the engine deck of my Panther, the civilian woman was lying on her back on the engine grilles, her clothes blackened by oil fumes and shredded by the shrapnel from the rockets. Her eyes were open and she was still breathing, but the air was escaping from her chest wounds in long hissing sounds. I lifted her and passed her down to civilians on the ground. The movement caused her a lot of pain, and she cried softly, with her eyes rolling back in her head. The Capo came and stood next to me, his hands on his hips.

'We have to move on,' he said, looking at the woman. 'The Jabos (*fighter-bombers*) are everywhere.'

'I promised to find this woman morphine,' I said. 'And we have none left.'

'She's dying.'

'She helped us find the path. She was useful to us.'

The Capo sighed, and called for his own Panther's medical kit. He took a morphine ampoule, and injected it into her arm. The woman moaned as it took effect, and opened her eyes. Her hands fumbled, and she dragged from her pocket a photograph which she thrust at me. I took it, and the woman became still. I guessed that her death was ten or twenty minutes away. At least she was dreaming.

I glanced at the photo she had given me. It showed a young woman of eighteen or twenty, the resemblance to the dying woman suggesting that it was her daughter. I frowned, and I put the picture in my tunic pocket, as more aircraft screamed in low above the trees, and the road that we had just passed over erupted in bursts of orange flame. I forgot about the photograph until much later.

—

Further along the track, the primitive road was scarred with craters from recent bombing, and our progress was slowed as we had to manoeuvre past these craters among the other traffic. In many cases, the craters were being bridged crudely with planks and logs, the labour being done by the doomed men that we called Hiwis.

The Hiwis were the *Hilfswilliger*: the 'willing helpers.' These were Soviet troops who had surrendered to our forces in the good years of 1941 and 1942, when it seemed to everyone that the German steamroller would crush the USSR flat. At the time, these men were faced with prison camps that consisted of great squares of barbed wire – no huts, no tents, no shelter of any kind. No food except the weeds, and no water except the rain. How many had we killed in those encampments, while our guards looked in through the wire as the Reds killed each other and ate the corpses raw? Was it a million, or – as some rumours said – was it actually two million that we starved to death? The Hiwis had volunteered to help the German armies as a way out of that hell, working for us as labourers, drivers and in other unarmed roles. Their reward was to keep living, to eat a ration every day and have a blanket at night. After Kursk in 1943, the Red soldiers became less prompt to surrender, and those that did were reluctant to work for us. They told us that the penalty for being captured was that their families would be sent to a Gulag in the Arctic.

Now the Hiwis in German territory were caught between two crushing forces. If they stopped helping us, they were of no further value, and did not deserve a ration. Their punishment would be a bullet or a noose. Their only consolation was that the Russians did not know they were taken prisoner, and so their families were safe. But if they were captured by the Russians now, their identities would eventually be uncovered – and both the Hiwis and their families would face a death sentence. What can a man do in such a situation, faced with such a choice? Some Hiwis killed themselves by whatever means they could find, while others continued to cooperate with our troops, hoping that in this way they could stave off their inevitable destiny. Their faces were set in masks of stress and fear, and their work was the work of condemned men, grim and methodical.

We came upon a gang of Hiwis which was some ten in number; men wearing a ragged mix of Russian and German uniforms and civilian clothing. These men had evidently survived years of their role, and were thin, with hollow eyes and shaved heads. They were hauling a 75mm PAK gun by hand out of a bomb crater as the gun crew simply stood and watched. The gun tractor was in a ditch beside the road, its engine pouring out smoke. As we passed by, other infantry ran past, shouting a warning that the Reds were close.

The trees to our left were bulldozed down, and as they fell we saw the green snout of A T34 pushing through them, barely fifty metres away. I could see another Red panzer behind it, and a squad of Red infantry too, clambering over the fallen tree trunks to get to us. There were screams from the civilians nearby, as, after so many years of being told about the Red beasts, the beasts themselves suddenly appeared in the flesh.

The Hiwis, meanwhile, ducked down into the bomb crater, leaving the PAK gun perched on the edge and the gun crew scrambling for their carbines. As the civilians stampeded away, I went down into the turret, ordered the Panther to halt, turn to face the Reds and fire as soon as the gunner was able.

It became a race to take the first shot. In panzer duels, the opening shot is often the deciding one if it strikes home; even if it does not destroy the enemy vehicle, it may damage the tracks or concuss the crew and buy precious seconds for a second shot. The task is to use a combination of the track differential to align the hull to the enemy tank, and the turret traverse to lay the shot itself, controlled by the gunner's final hydraulics.

An oddity of our Panthers was that only the gunner himself could traverse the turret – the commander had no traversing pedals of his own, and for those breathless seconds, while the gunner rotated the great turret left and right with his face against the padded rim of the gun sight, the gunner was the most important man in the machine. The Panther turret traversed slowly, but to our advantage we were already stationary, while the T34 was still labouring over the collapsed trees towards us.

Our shot rang out, the tracer flew in its red line – and at that range, our 75mm round punched directly through the T34's turret, below the gun mantle. Through my periscope, I saw the Red panzer recoil from the impact, and the machine crashed into an oak tree, uprooting it. The Red infantry spread around the crippled panzer without faltering, and even when the T34's turret exploded off the hull in a column of flame, then came hurtling down to crush several infantrymen as it hit the ground – even then, they kept advancing on us.

We fired from the bow machine gun, bringing down many of the Reds, and at the same time my gunner was sighting on the second T34, which was scrabbling over the wrecked trees in its eagerness to get at us. As its hull rose, we fired at its exposed belly plate – but our shot went wide as the panzer crashed down horizontally again, and we succeeded only in deflecting off the sloped front armour in a cloud of metal particles. My gunner cursed, and my loader worked like a devil to get the next round into the chamber – but as he closed the breech block, that second T34 opened up on us.

I had expected a tracer round, or high explosive intended to tear off our tracks, but what erupted from the T34's turret was a long, straight spurt of burning liquid, an absolute torrent of fire, which spurted through the trees towards us, the splashes catching one of the Red infantry as he scrambled to get clear, and setting the man on fire. The man's comrades made no attempt to help him as he burned, but scattered through the trees away from the fire, moving around to our flank.

This T34 was a Flammpanzer (*flamethrower tank*) fitted with a fire projector that resembled a normal gun, and its burst of flame caused so much smoke among the trees that it was impossible for a few seconds to see the vehicle itself. My gunner muttered to himself, his face pressed against the gun sight, making estimates of where the machine would exit the smoke, and traversing a fraction to lay his shot there. I told the loader to have a high-explosive round ready next, intending to blow away the flame tube on the enemy panzer. To our right, the Red infantry was exchanging shots with the PAK gunners and a squad of German troops who had come out from the forest – but of the thousands who must be hiding nearby in the trees, only about fifty came forward ready to defend the Kessel.

As I looked back through the periscope at the smoke, the Flammpanzer crashed out of the flames and charged towards us, spurting a new line of incendiary liquid that flew wildly around the forest as the panzer swayed between the trees. The fire shot past us, but I knew that if the liquid hit our rear deck, the flames would immediately pour through the engine grilles and blow up our engine in an instant. We in the crew compartment would be reduced to ashes if we could not escape the hull in time. Already I could smell the stench of the Russian incendiary fuel, and feel the intense heat from its flames, even through our armour plate.

Our round was fired in a hurry, and struck the edge of the T34's turret, glancing off into the trees without penetrating at that oblique angle. The Flammpanzer lurched forward, traversing its turret to aim its fire directly at us, and elevating its projector tube to make sure that its flames poured down onto us from above. The Red commander did not get that chance. Our high explosive round exploded on the front of his turret, and, as I had hoped, the detonation wrenched off the thin flame projector, sending it spinning off into the trees, trailing a ribbon of flames. Liquid began to gush out from the shattered gun mantle, cascading down onto the front hull – and, as the T34 began to reverse back into the trees to escape us, we landed another high explosive round in the same place.

The effect was immediate. The shrapnel must have set off the panzer's liquid fuel reservoir for its flame gun, because the turret hatch blew open and a vertical blast of fire shot up into the air. All of us in the Panther crew muttered thanks that this fate was theirs, and not ours. What would it be like in the T34's cramped hull, as the entire supply of fuel exploded, sending that tower of flames thirty or forty metres high? In seconds, the flames collapsed down onto the panzer, and it was enveloped in its own fire, wedged between burning trees and sending spirals of debris out into the forest as it blew itself to pieces.

The battle was not over yet. The Red infantrymen, seeing their panzers destroyed, began to retreat, but kept up a barrage of machine gun fire at our troops as they withdrew. I saw that, passing the bomb crater with the PAK gun perched on its lip, the Reds shouted and gestured in triumph as they discovered the gang of Hiwi men sheltering inside there, unarmed. Our troops began to hold their fire – perhaps conserving their precious ammunition, but also, I suspected as I watched, waiting to see what the Russians would do with their fellow countrymen in the crater. I climbed out onto the rear deck to take a clear look around, and saw no more enemy panzers approaching from any direction. The burning Flammpanzer was still erupting in orange flames.

I saw that the Russians were surrounding the crater, putting grenades down the barrel of the PAK gun to disable it, and firing their machine pistols down into the pit. I could just see the bodies of the Hiwis shuddering as they were torn up by the bullets fired by their compatriots. I shouted to one of our infantry on the ground, a young Feldwebel, to fire on the Reds and save the Hiwis, but it was too late. Their task completed, the Red infantry ran back into the trees towards their own lines, yelling and whooping in Russian.

The whole forest fell quiet for a few moments, apart from the hiss and roar of the burning T34 in the trees. I asked the infantry Feldwebel why his men had not done more to help the Hiwis in the crater. He shrugged.

'We have too many Hiwis in the Kessel already,' he said. 'They're becoming a problem. If the Reds want to solve the problem for us, that's fine.'

As we skirted the crater and moved on, I glanced down into the pit. The Hiwis were jumbled in a heap at the bottom, their bodies still smoking from the bullet impacts. The damaged PAK gun was pushed in on top of them, and the scene was abandoned as the columns moved on to the West.

——

In the Halbe Kessel, the dead lay where they fell, or were dragged to one side of the track and left among the trees. I saw some bodies being thrown into marshes, and some being dropped into bomb craters. In my time inside the Kessel, I never saw a grave being dug or the earth being smoothed over a corpse.

Our journey onward was slow, in the gathering shadows of the late evening. In this warm, dusty air, the sights, sounds and smells of the Kessel were stamped on my senses with a dreadful clarity. Inside the Panther turret, the air was heated and rank with fuel and explosive, the transmission churning in the hull floor below the turret cage. We dumped our spent 75mm shell cases from the collection box below the gun, throwing them out of the loader's hatch in the turret rear, and left all the hatches open in an attempt to ventilate the compartment. The Panther's lack of a loader's roof hatch made the attempt difficult. With my torso up through the commander's cupola, I could see the two SS King Tigers lumbering behind us, still carrying their load of exhausted SS troopers. On our panzer, every centimetre was taken up with wounded men who had pleaded for a ride, who lay bandaged and clenching their fists, even across the turret roof. Even our sloped front plate, with its pocks and dents from enemy rounds that did not penetrate, was draped with men holding on by their feet to the front track covers.

Explosions were all around us, rumbling in from the perimeter of the Kessel, and random artillery shells exploded in the tree canopy sporadically. We had to bulldoze our way past a row of Luftwaffe trucks which were abandoned in the road, fuel siphons still hanging from their gasoline tanks. In the midst of this great crisis, these trucks were loaded with paintings and silverware that seemed to be taken from churches, the contents tipped out by those passing on foot and cast aside in their search for the necessities of fuel, water and ammunition. A large crater beside the track was full of corpses, troops and civilians, adults and children, thrown in without order or ceremony. The smell of decay made my stomach bunch as we passed. In an area of marsh in a forest clearing, the green surface of the bog was dotted with vehicles that had been pushed in away from the road. Among them, a superb Jagdpanther tank-hunter vehicle was sunk up to its roof, with birds already settling on its cupola.

We glimpsed through the trees an area of open meadowland – in which an American Flying Fortress bomber was crash-landed, with its belly sunk into the ground and its tail fin as high as the trees. The meadow was being shelled, and although we were tempted to explore the plane wreck for possible fuel or supplies, we watched as the shell bursts straddled the great aircraft, and then hit it, blowing its fuselage to pieces in towers of flying metal. The shell bursts moved into the trees among us, and for a minute the forest was full of the screams of civilians between the detonating rounds. When the barrage moved away from us, it left a line of cars on fire, dead civilians scattered in the undergrowth, and then the columns of vehicles and walkers began moving on again. All around us, civilians and troops begged for a ride, for water, food, medicines and directions, nobody knowing exactly where their friends or their units were. Some troops remained in units or groups with their officers, but many were now making their way west without leaders, combining together as the journey demanded.

Money seemed to have no value in the Kessel. I witnessed a staff officer offering a wallet full of Reichsmarks to a Hanomag driver in return for a ride; the offer was rejected with a curse, but the driver took on a civilian couple who paid with a gold ring. The only viable currencies were gold, water, gasoline, food and morphine – these were the things that the people of the Kessel held dear to their hearts. Order had broken down, and discipline, where it was enforced, was brutal and arbitrary.

At one stage in this sector, we passed what appeared to be a panzer maintenance workshop set up beside a barn. I saw first the large steel gantry which was used to lift turrets and engines from our panzers: a tall steel frame on wheels which rolled over the top of even the heaviest panzer. I was desperately relieved to see this maintenance site, as the final drive transmission in my Panther was in its final stage of service. The huge power chain only lasted for eight hundred kilometres, and mine had passed nine hundred in the entry into the Kessel. The steel casing in the forward hull was leaking oil badly, and I could hear the mesh slipping in the gears as the driver sought to control it. If the system jammed in combat, it would surely finish us all.

Did we have time to replace it, if a replacement was, by some miracle, available here?

I saw a Panther already parked under the gantry crane, and three mechanics standing on its forward hull, looking down at the transmission cover. I knew the procedure well: the forward transmission on the Panther, positioned in the front hull driving the front wheels, required the mechanics to remove a rectangular plate in the hull roof above the radio operator and driver's heads. This plate, part of the armour sheet, was unbolted and then lifted clear with the crane. The mechanics would swarm into the exposed hull, freeing the entire transmission from its mountings and then lifting that out as well. The new final drive would be lowered in, the machinery so bulky that it had to be swung down through the space a millimetre at a time to ensure that it passed through.

While this was going on, the engine deck at the rear would be opened and the armoured grilles taken out. The complete Maybach engine would be hoisted out by the crane, and a new one installed in the armoured box inside the engine bay. The whole process could be completed by skilled mechanics in a day, leaving the Panther ready to travel another 800km before the entire engine and transmission had to be replaced again.

And so, when I saw the gantry crane in place over this Panther beside the barn, and the three mechanics standing there on the hull, I expected this operation to be underway; but I saw no sign of the spare parts which were usually strewn around the service area. There was only the Panther, with the crane overhead, and the men standing on the deck. Then I realised that the men were connected to the crane, with lines stretching from their necks to the steel girders. The men, in fact, had ropes around their necks: ropes strung up to the crane.

I shielded my eyes to see what was happening there. The Panther under the crane revved up, spewing out fumes, and then moved backward rapidly a few metres. The men on the front deck were left dangling, their feet jerking and their bodies convulsing as they were hung on the ropes. The Panther commander turned to look at them – and then turned to face forwards, as the panzer revved again and moved away down onto the forest track. The Panther bore the markings of the SS Panzer Corps.

Time was pressing, and we could not stop to examine the scene. But as we passed, I did observe that the three men, swaying on their nooses as their bodies went limp, were in Wehrmacht panzer mechanics uniforms: the oil-stained overalls I had seen so many times. Around each man's neck was a placard, with writing which I glimpsed before we moved off:

This man helped the Reds
By refusing to help the Waffen SS

When I glanced back, the gantry of the crane was full of ravens.

The Kessel was not the place to make protests or complaints, or to debate the question of martial law. It was the place to keep moving, and keep your mouth shut, and listen to the groans of your transmission, not the sounds of the wounded or dying.

—

By shouting out requests for directions, we made our way through the gathering gloom into an area where panzers and other armoured vehicles were dispersed among ancient oak trees. There were a trio of Hetzer tank-destroyers, these useful little vehicles being worked on by their crews, and a unit of Panzer IV vehicles. The Panzer IVs were in bad shape: their mesh armour screens buckled and torn, and their engine hatches emitting brown smoke. One was being towed by a captured T34 chassis used as a tractor with no turret. That sturdy Russian panzer had travelled how many kilometres, and changed hands how many times – and it served whoever drove it reliably, with no complaints.

We edged past these vehicles, still with our load of wounded and trailing our column of followers on foot, until a solitary Kettenhund (*military police officer*) directed us forward to a clearing point where information would be available. By the time we finally pulled in to this point, darkness was gathering, and our engines were overheating badly again. The SS King Tigers moved away at walking pace, led by guides on foot who had cable phones connected to the drivers, seeking their SS Panzer Corps unit which had its elements in the forest to the North. The Capo and his gunner went to confer with the other panzer officers. We on my panzer opened the engine grilles and checked over the Maybach as it gurgled and clattered in the twilight.

All around us, people on foot were preparing to pass the night. People's behaviour was becoming unpredictable, and it seemed that many wanted to drown out their fears. Among all the cries of the wounded, the sound of improvised drinking parties was clear on the breeze, complete with mournful singing and the chinking of bottles.

Some men and women were going into the shadows as couples, and the sounds of their copulation were clear to hear: the sound of people desperate to find some distraction, some suspension from the Kessel. One woman, a Luftwaffe Flak worker, did not bother to find a discreet place, but accepted a Waffen SS man on the ground between the trees, her eyes blank as she stared up over his shoulder. We shook our heads at her audacity, but truly, who could blame her – because who knew how long their life would last, or their body would remain unscarred? A parachute flare ignited high above us, and its lunar light showed the whole scene in sharp relief. Behind the lucky SS man, others were waiting to take his place.

The Reich had come to this condition now.

How much further would it fall?

It was around eleven pm, and the sky was at times as bright as day, as the flares drifted over the trees or lines of tracer twisted overhead to strike the forest some distance away. The sound of combat along the perimeter of the Kessel was loud now, and it seemed that the Reds were drawing the noose tighter all the time. Groups of wounded soldiers came limping through our positions regularly, pleading for medical attention, or knots of civilians pushing their wounded on hand carts, telling us in wild voices that the Russians were getting closer, always closer. One civilian woman shot herself with a pistol, and her dead body lay among the trees, near the brazen Luftwaffe girl and the eager SS men.

The Capo returned, and with him the leaders of the other armoured units drawn up in this part of the forest. They stood near our Panther for a few minutes, talking in low voices, and then dispersed. The Capo called us together, away from the milling foot soldiers, in the channel between our two Panthers, with the great dish wheels on either side of us. Our drivers ran their hands instinctively along the track links as they listened, mentally assessing the tension of the track length. A green flare exploded above the treetops, casting a jagged light across us as it floated downward.

'The Kessel is small, but crowded,' the Capo said, without emotion. 'There could be a hundred thousand troops inside here, and maybe twenty or thirty thousand civilians. The Reds have fresh troops stationed around us, with new armour, and they're pushing in all the time. In one day, or two days, the Kessel will surely fall.'

He looked between the panzers at a group of civilian women and children, asleep in the carcass of a truck that had become stuck between two trees. The children were asleep on top of the women, their faces lit by the swaying green flare light. With that colouring, their bodies already resembled corpses.

'Those in the pocket who can break out, will break out now. At midnight.'

'In forty-five minutes, Herr Leutnant?' I said. 'Our fuel –'

'In forty-five minutes,' the Capo nodded. 'We will fight through a place called Halbe, that is the village immediately to the West. The Reds hold it, but we have a lot of panzers concentrated in a small zone. We will punch through Halbe, into the flat land on the other side, and cross the North-South autobahn at Baruth, or near there. After that, it is forty or fifty kilometres to the positions of the Twelfth Army, who are ready to receive us. We will pass through the Twelfth Army corridor and reach the river Elbe. We know that the Elbe is held by Americans on the west bank. We will be taken prisoner in the West, in the American zone. We know why this must be done. Germany needs us after the war ends, and if we are captured by the Russians we will not see Germany again.'

The green flare overhead caught in the treetops and set light to the foliage. At the same time, there was a shriek of descending shells, and we threw ourselves flat between the Panthers, trusting to their steel to fend off the explosions. Looking up, I saw the truck full of women and children fly into pieces, with bodies whirling through the air in the flashing light. I pressed my face into the ground and dug my fingers into the earth, as the Panthers rocked in the bombardment and the stink of explosive and smoke enveloped us, the screams and cries of the wounded over the echoes of the detonations.

When that was over, and the artillery rounds stopped falling, I stood up, unwilling to face the sight of the blown-apart truck. The Capo was already on his feet, staring at the wreckage. The civilians were dismembered, lying in dark pools in the green light of another flare. Nearby, the Luftwaffe woman and her SS lovers were also dead, their bodies jumbled together in a smouldering pile, her eyes still blank and open.

We started the panzer engines.

—

The way to the breakout point was marked by Kettenhund (*military police*) men and panzer officers, holding masked flashlights and keeping all pedestrian traffic off the forest tracks, by force if necessary. We saw one Kettenhund kick an encroaching infantry man out of our way – and then shoot him with his MP40 when the man fought his way back onto the road. Whole carts and wagons were tipped over to clear the roadways, their civilian owners watching us mutely in the light of the overhead flares and the flashes of explosions from the perimeters. We passed under an oak tree burning like a brazier, surrounded by the bodies of wounded troops who had been sheltering under it when a shell struck.

Our way was lit again by the flames of a burning aircraft which scraped the treetops and then crashed to our right, in a ball of flames that resembled the morning sun. We followed two of the Hetzer destroyers – and when one of them was hit by a falling tree and immobilised, we bulldozed it out of the way with our front plate and simply carried on. Behind us was a jumble of armoured elements, all racing for the breakout point, and behind that we knew that there was a dense column of foot soldiers and civilians, people in wagons, cars and trucks, all desperate to follow the armoured spearhead through Halbe and out to the West.

The plan for the breakout was crude – it had to be, because the Reds were crushing the pocket around us, minute by minute, metre by metre. The first blows would be struck by the King Tigers of the SS Panzer Corps, supported by the remaining armour, artillery and Panzergrenadiers from the 21st Panzer.

'The SS boys are desperate to be the first ones out of the Kessel,' the Capo had said to us with a wry smile. 'They know there's no prison for them – not even in Siberia. Any SS who falls into Red hands is shot or clubbed to death. We can rely on them to lead the way.'

I could see the flashes of our artillery firing through the trees on either side of the road. The gunners were under orders to fire off all their rounds, then smash their gun breech blocks and race for the breakthrough point on foot; the fuel tanks of their trucks had been drained to provide gasoline for the panzers. Ahead of us was the Capo's Panther, his exhausts trailing flames, and beyond him the stretch of open country that led to Halbe itself. I could see that fighting was already erupting out there, beyond the screen of the forest. Bursts of flame, drifting flares and the starburst explosions of rockets lit up the open heath in spasms of light. I slid down into the cupola, sealed the hatch, and held on as we lurched out of the final forest track out into the heath.

Through the periscopes, I saw the church tower of Halbe town, illuminated against a curtain of flames. Whatever was happening in that small town, the place resembled a medieval inferno, full of sparks and fires. Our Panther rolled across the heathland, smashing apart stationary cars and trucks that were strewn in the open. The flares overhead gave a light that varied from dusk to bright sunshine, making my eyes constantly adapt and readapt to the intensity. In one such flash, I saw the Capo's Panther run over a motorcycle and sidecar, and send the whole machine flying through the air behind its tracks. The motorcycle span towards us, blocking my vision as it crashed onto our turret before disappearing. We slammed down into a sudden defile – and I cursed out a prayer that this was not an anti-tank ditch. As we clawed up the other side, I saw tracer flash past us, and then we were hit twice on the glacis plate as we levelled out. There were Red PAK guns down there around the village, and the decision for us was whether to halt and fire on them, or to keep moving and present a rapid target. The Capo had no doubts: I saw his Panther sway and lurch as he approached the town in a ragged zig-zag, with tracer flying past him at each turn.

With a few hundred metres to go, we had to slow down to pick our way between craters and ditches which would trap us for sure. In this zone, we came to a King Tiger that was immobile in a crater, its nose slumped down and evidently stuck fast. Its huge gun barrel was elevated so that it could fire on the PAKs, and it was maintaining a storm of fire on those positions. As we went past this stranded panzer, I saw it struck on the side of the turret by a tracer round – and then by another. The whole seventy-tonne machine lurched, its hatches flying open and emitting towers of flames, until one final explosion from inside lifted the entire turret off the hull, and sent a sphere of red flames boiling up above us.

Lit by this fire, we presented an easy target, but within a few seconds we were literally on top of the surviving Russian PAK guns, too close for them to fire over open sights.

The PAKs were dug in along a series of emplacements before the town, and the advance wave of King Tigers had already mauled them badly. In the chaotic light of the flares, I saw that several guns had been run over and crushed by panzers, their barrels and wheels reduced to a jumble of steel, and their crews dismembered around them. One PAK was still intact and surrounded by living men, and we halted with a great screech of metal to let our gunner lay his sight on it. At a range of fifty metres, we used one high explosive round to demolish the emplacement. Some of the Red gunners, outlined against the flames from the town behind them, raised their hands in surrender. My gunner shot them down with his coaxial MG, and we rolled forward into the outskirts of the town itself.

The open heath gave way to a series of farm buildings, and then the first outlying houses of Halbe, at some distance from the town itself. The Capo's Panther was already moving between the farm units, and ahead of him I could make out one of the King Tigers which had spearheaded the breakout, its profile stark against the flames. All around, shells were detonating, knocking huge pieces out of the farmsteads and rocking us with their blast. In the swirling light, we almost collided with a Panzer IV which was immobile beside a barn. Peering through the periscopes, it was difficult to make out what was happening around us, with so much smoke and dust. I put my head up out of the cupola to try to see the way ahead.

The roar of explosions and flames surged over me.

The Panzer IV in front of us had shed its tracks, which were looped around it in ragged pieces. The panzer crew were clambering out on the hull, gesturing to me to accept them on board. As I shouted to them to climb on, though, figures emerged from trenches around us: figures of men in Red Army padded jackets, and they began to swarm over the Panzer IV. In moments, the panzer crew were shot down – one man who jumped clear being stabbed through the neck with a bayonet by one of these Ivan panzer hunters. My hull gunner and main gunner both fired their MGs, and shot the men on the panzer to pieces – both the Soviets and the dead bodies of the panzer crew. The adversaries lay jumbled on top of each other, in the light of the flames, their blood mingling on the armour plate.

As soon as this danger was overcome – Red panzers burst in among us.

These were not the ordinary T34s, I saw immediately, as one of these monsters appeared through the smoke and began to traverse its squat, oblong turret onto us. These were Josef Stalin types – the equal of a King Tiger, with a slow but fatal main gun more powerful even than an 88mm. I gave the bearing of one of them to my gunner.

'JS!' my gunner muttered in my headphones, and I felt the turret twitch as he traversed our 75mm onto the Russian. I dropped back inside of the turret, where peering out through the periscopes I could barely see the Stalin, about one hundred metres distant, shrouded in the smoke. That massive Red panzer would normally stand back and pick its enemies off at distances of two kilometres or more – but in the dark and smoke, it needed to come to close quarters to be able to see its prey. Its colossal main gun was gradually turning onto us, but our traverse was quicker, and our driver aided it by using the track differential to swivel our hull so that our gun came into alignment more rapidly. While the Ivan turret was still turning, we fired. The round deflected off its armour and disappeared into the smoke. Beside me, my 75mm loader worked like a grim dervish on the breech while the gun fumes filled the turret. We fired again. I blinked, wiped my eyes and stared at the JS.

'That round,' I said. 'Is it –'

'Yes,' the gunner muttered, squinting through his gun sight. 'It's stuck in the armour.'

Our 75mm projectile was sticking out of the JS turret armour, still smoking, like the horn on a devil.

'Reverse!'

We slammed backward, crashing through the wall of a barn, as the JS fired on us. Its round flashed in front of us, and flew off across the open heath towards the Spree Forest. We were at point bank range with this Stalin panzer, blinded by smoke, in a zone that we had no knowledge of. The only thing we knew for certain was that we had to get through the town of Halbe, and this Stalin was barring our path.

The Capo's Panther was nowhere to be seen – and where were our King Tigers? How would we break past these huge Ivan machines into the town, and out to the West? Every thought, every breath was punctuated by the detonation of mortar rounds exploding between us and the Stalins. If we could not break past them, the Kessel exit would be sealed again and its hundred thousand inhabitants would meet a savage destiny.

The Russian JS panzer was notoriously slow to reload its huge gun, having, we believed, a two-part shell system in which the projectile and propellant were loaded separately, as on a battleship. In the time it took, my loader replenished our breech again, and I ordered my gunner to fire on the Stalin which had shot at us – but to hit him in the running gear, not the hull or turret. It was a difficult shot, in the drifting smoke, with only the front of the Stalin's track visible as a target. We fired once – and the round deflected off the edge of the glacis by the track.

We were reloaded and primed in seconds, and our second shot blew the right front track clean off the Stalin's drive wheel, making the machine rock on its axis. Before its crew could react, I ordered our driver to charge the Stalin, and to veer around so that we were at its rear, where the armour plate was thinner over the engine. With mortar rounds bursting around us, we crashed out of the barn and over to the Stalin's right, then slowed and rotated around so that our gun was pointing at the Red panzer's back plate. I saw the Stalin try to heave itself around on one track, but this was slow and our gunner was faster on his final traverse.

Our precious armour-piercing shell smashed into the Stalin's thin, back armour. The light from the overhead flares was so clear that I could see our round pierce the metal in a spray of dislodged fragments. The round deflected off something inside there, and came shooting up vertically out of the engine grilles, followed by a plume of sparks. The grilles flew apart, and a flash of flame lit up the whole Stalin, turning to oily smoke which coiled in tentacles around the vehicle as it shuddered and tried to move.

We began to reverse from it, conserving our ammunition, but that Stalin crew was not done with us. As we turned to drive past the wrecked machine, I saw its hatches open and men climb out, calmly and orderly: five men, some armed with machine pistols. Our hull gunner fired and knocked two of them down, but the armed men dodged towards us, getting so close to our flank that I lost sight of them beside the Panther. We began to accelerate away – but immediately crashed through the smoke into an earth mound which blocked our backward progress. Our cursing reached a crescendo of obscenity as our dish wheels slid while we tried to reverse over the mound, our hull up in the air and our tracks throwing out earth as our weight took us back down. As we landed with a crash, I heard the screech of our engine cut out and die.

Our Panther had stalled, and we were stationary.

None of us needed to curse our driver – he knew exactly what to do. He worked the starter lever, trying to engage the start motor, making the system whine but not catch, each sound tearing at our hearts. I saw our loader's eyes fill with tears, and I had no words to console him. Were we now to be stranded here, and forced to join the helpless swarms of people on foot rushing through the maelstrom of Halbe?

'Please...' our gunner said. 'Come on, please...'

'It won't catch,' our driver muttered. 'It won't –'

I heard noises on the rear deck of the Panther.

Were they German troops, climbing aboard in the middle of the battlefield?

I peered through the rear periscope, and caught sight of a Russian tank crewman in his ribbed helmet, smashing at our engine grilles with the butt of his machine pistol. The *verdamm* Reds wanted vengeance on us for destroying their fine Stalin panzer. I fired my pistol through the small port in the turret rear intended for this purpose, but the angle was wrong, and without engine power we could only turn the turret slowly with the hand crank. If the Reds put one bullet into our fuel pipes, or one grenade under the grilles, our Panther would never start again. I slid open my cupola hatch, took my MP40 from the turret wall, and pointed the gun out over the top. I realised it was no use shooting like that – my bullets would surely go through our own grilles. With no choice, I heaved myself out, and came face to face with a Red tank crewman, who was trying to prime a flare pistol, pointing it down at the engine covers.

I shot him, and he tumbled off the deck – but his comrade was on top of me. Unarmed, the man smashed me in the face with his fist, and I tasted thick blood in my mouth. I shot at him wildly, and saw him jump from the Panther onto the earth. Down there, a gang of our troops leaped forward – not only troops, but women too, armed with rifles and pistols. They set upon this man and cut him to pieces with shots and blows – until one woman, armed with a civilian shotgun, administered the final blast to his face. At the same time, our engine rumbled and caught, and the Panther came to life again under me.

'Comrade, take us with you!' the ground troops shouted over the din.

I could not deny the ground soldiers and civilians the chance to ride with us – the approach to Halbe would be murderous on the back of a panzer, but if they wished to take the danger, so be it. And their close-quarters protection against marauding Russian infantry would be welcome. With this clutch of half a dozen armed fighters on our rear deck, I climbed back into the turret. We rounded the earth embankment and moved off towards Halbe itself in search of our other panzers and the route to the West.

Coming through the outlying farm buildings, with me peering through the periscopes from inside the turret, I saw quickly how our SS King Tigers were engaged. The lights of flames and the parachute flares were still bright, and in that flickering glow I saw that our heavy panzers were fighting another row of Stalins. These Red panzers were dug into the ground on the edge of the village itself, with only their turrets above the earth. I could see three of them, with their block-shaped turrets black against the flames behind them. Our King Tigers were shooting them up from a range of less than one kilometre, blowing up clouds of soil as their high-explosive shells exploded around the emplaced Stalins. One Tiger was evidently firing armour-piercing, and I saw the tracer shells corkscrew off from the side of a Stalin's turret in the drifting smoke. On the other side of the Tigers, I thought I could make out the Capo's Panther, behind a ridge, firing intermittently at the Stalins.

Behind those few Red panzers, the town of Halbe stood in flames, with artillery rounds exploding over it in starbursts that sent roof tiles and chimneys whirling for hundreds of metres. I guessed that bombardment was the last of our artillery using its ammunition to break up the Soviet positions in the town. The Russian artillery, though, was now laying down a thick screen of explosions in front of the town, daring us to run the gauntlet of shrapnel even if we could defeat the Stalins. I did not anticipate that our Panthers would be of great use in this initial fight against the Stalins – that would take the King Tigers. Besides, I didn't need to count our ammunition – I knew it well enough: barely twenty rounds of armour-piercing remaining, and ten rounds of high-explosive. That would need to last until we were through the town, over the land to the West and inside the Twelfth Army corridor.

I kept my Panther concealed in the rubble of a collapsed farm house, where the rafters and slates covered our profile, and, with our riders still cowering on our rear deck, I considered how to approach the town.

I could see four King Tigers in all, firing on the three Stalins, their higher rate of fire undermined as an advantage by the ultra-low position of the Red panzers in the ground. The Tigers were having no success, and they were taking hits on their front plates from those massive battleship guns in the Stalin machines. One such hit struck a King Tiger on the gun mantle, and I saw in an instant that the tracer shell deflected down and hit the deck hatches under the barrel. A hatch flew off into the air, and then a jet of sparks erupted from the deck. I shuddered to think of that Soviet warhead screaming around the inside of our panzer, ricocheting off the interior walls and carving a path through any human body that it touched. I had looked inside the hulks of many destroyed panzers – ours and the Russians – and I knew what the process did to flesh and bone. The

King Tiger's turret hatches blew open – and in a moment its ammunition exploded, sending a helix of flame up from the open vents. Even as the panzer was enveloped in its burning gasoline, the other King Tigers took their revenge, focussing all their fire for a furious ten seconds on one of the embedded Stalins.

My gunner chuckled to himself. With his telescopic sight, he had a better view than me – but even I could see the Stalin hit repeatedly by three, then four shells, until a great scab of metal broke away from the turret and span off across the ground. The broken shell of the turret exploded, throwing the crew members up into the air amid sparks and flames. They had scarcely fallen to earth before the King Tigers turned their fire to the second Stalin, which was hit immediately in the gun barrel where it joined the turret.

That Stalin's barrel slumped, and the huge machine began to reverse back out of its low emplacement. The overhead flares turned to orange and green, and in this lurid illumination we saw the Stalin reverse a few metres, exposing its upper hull to our Tigers as it went back up the gradient. One 88mm round punctured the forward hull, and another ripped open the engine deck as it rose into the air. The Stalin slumped back down into its trench, with crew men beginning to drag themselves out of the hatches, their clothing and helmets on fire. I thought the Tigers had finished with them – but one of the Waffen SS gunners insisted on firing a high explosive round which exploded centrally on the Stalin.

My gunner chuckled again.

The Red crewmen climbing out of the hatches were severed in half by the explosion – their torsos blasted completely away, leaving only the stumps of their bodies jammed in the hatch openings. Its escape routes blocked, and its hull shot to pieces, the Stalin began to burn.

The third Stalin panzer was outnumbered now by three to one, but still it kept firing on the King Tigers. I had to admire its commander when, with 88mm rounds smashing off its turret, the panzer reared up and burst out of its dug-in emplacement onto the open ground itself. There was to be no retreat for this hero of the Soviet

Union, even if nobody ever knew his name or his actions. He was going down defiantly, taking his machine and his crew with him.

That was achieved in a few seconds, as the Stalin began to race towards the three King Tigers, clearly intent on ramming one of them. The Tigers shot his tracks off with high explosive, and, as the Stalin careered sideways across the heath, they stood silently and watched as the Red panzer crashed into a crater, flipped over slowly, and came to rest upside down, its turret in the earth now and its wheels in the sky. Flames licked around it slowly, but the King Tigers were already moving towards it, then past it - and then their lumbering profiles moved into the outskirts of the town itself.

My Panther followed, tucking in behind the Capo's Panther as he too emerged from his concealment and joined the column. Behind us, I saw through the periscopes in the glow of the flares and burning vehicles that hundreds of people were already following us closely – troops, Wehrmacht, SS and civilians, in cars, trucks on foot and on Hanomags – as our breakout column slowly pushed ahead into the chaos of Halbe town.

—

The Battle at Halbe

Halbe was once like a thousand small towns dotted across Germany: timbered houses, merchants' halls, a market square, a church, a simple railroad station. Its buildings had been the homes of well-to-do farmers and dealers, neat and square. On this late April night, it was illuminated by parachute flares, and by the flames erupting from its tiled roofs and timber window shutters.

I went up out of the cupola to see better and to guide my driver. The first thing that I saw, in the gardens of the houses on the outskirts, were the bodies of dead civilians strewn about everywhere – twenty or thirty people of all ages, who seemed to have been caught by shell fire. We passed these pale bodies, and followed the other panzers between the houses into the main street of the town.

As we halted there, I took in the scene.

Our King Tigers were positioned along the main street, their turrets level with the upper windows of the old buildings. The Capo's Panther was in front of me. From behind us, German troops and civilians were starting to stream through the gaps in the houses, and emerge into this main street, huddling close to the panzers. Some troops, those who retained combat discipline and were armed, moved slowly along the building frontages, checking for signs of Red infantry. These men exchanged fire with Russians in the first houses – shooting through the windows and throwing in grenades to clear them out. Each shot and explosion made the civilians huddle closer to the panzers – and not only the civilians;

many German troops were unarmed and simply following us as non-combatants, with no interest in sharing the fighting. These men – some walking wounded, but many able-bodied – let their comrades do the dangerous work while they stayed back in the shadow of the panzers.

Overhead, the drifting parachute flares began to burn themselves out, and no more were fired from beyond the town. This meant that the Reds knew we had captured the place, and they wanted to give us no advantage of light. The fighting in the houses took place in a renewed darkness, lit by flames and gun flashes, with men scrambling among the wreckage of the house fronts and doorways.

I saw the German infantry drag the remaining Reds out by their collars and belts, throwing them onto the cobblestones and surrounding them. To save ammunition, they killed the prisoners with their rifle butts, boots and with entrenching spades, clubbing and stabbing them to death. The civilians peered around the panzers to witness this killing – old men, women and children too. By the time this was done, this end of the street was littered with mangled Red corpses, visible in the fires of the burning buildings.

With the street secured, it was the stage to move on and through the town to the West. Looking behind us, I could make out a great river of people on foot: horses, carts and unarmoured vehicles, bulging up in this bottle neck of the main street. As the King Tigers moved ahead, screened by the combatant infantry, our two Panthers moved off slowly after them, and the mass of people to our rear followed too. At first, they stayed behind our Panther, but then in a few metres many of them ran past us, weaving between the bodies along the street, stumbling from one panzer to the next – until the whole street was packed with thousands of people on foot, all rushing towards the other side of the town.

When this surge of people was at its height, and the street was a dense, moving river of human heads, swirling forwards between the panzers like islands in a flood – at this point, the Red artillery opened fire on the town.

Of course, the Reds had their observers hidden nearby, communicating the situation to their commanders, and they had plotted the coordinates of the main street carefully in advance. Even so, the bombardment that they unleashed on the street was merciless and devastating in its accuracy.

The first shell exploded behind us, throwing a large number of people into the air and sending broken cobble stones whirling along the narrow transit like missiles. The shells burst in a calculated line going forward, from the rear of the column towards the front. The explosions ripped the tightly-packed crowd apart, sending some bodies crashing against the house fronts and others through the shattered windows of the storefronts. I caught sight of a soldier and a civilian woman, blasted off their feet and blown into a shop, where they lay among the burning goods while the building caught fire around them.

My driver shouted a question to me.

'Shall I advance at speed, Herr Feldwebel? To reach the other end of the street?'

I tried to see in front of us.

The King Tigers were accelerating – and as they picked up speed to get away from the explosions, they struck and crushed many people on foot around them. Some bodies were thrown sideways, while others were dragged under the huge metal treads, or simply disappeared beneath the King Tiger's massive hull. At the same time, the artillery increased even more in intensity, with rounds bursting in the street and against the buildings every few seconds, both explosive rounds and incendiary rockets.

At this point, the road in front of my Panther exploded in a spray of white fire, a light so intense that it hurt my eyes to look at it even through the periscopes. I recognised this as a magnesium or phosphorous shell, and I felt the heat surge over our panzer as the fire grew. The burning chemical expanded in the air, creating huge spirals that grew to a height of several metres against the frontage of the house beside the street. The building began to burn, as the white substance dripped like a molten waterfall down its surface.

There were civilians in the building, and I saw some of them try to jump out through windows away from the fire, but the blazing chemical kept expanding, and caught the people as they leaped. They fell, completely on fire, into the street - and the entire house began to collapse on top of them where they lay.

In front of us was an armoured car – an eight-wheeled command vehicle – and this car reversed suddenly, away from the flames, hitting our front plate with a substantial impact. I heard the car rev and its wheels scream as they span on the cobbles, but my radio man called up to me that the vehicle's rear fender was jammed under our front plate. There was a flash from the car itself, and flames began to spread up its angular surface. Its crew began to jump from the upper hatches. It seemed that the armoured car's fuel tank was split and leaking, and the gasoline was pouring onto the street under our panzer. Shells were bursting around us too, and the front of the burning building was collapsing into the street. I told my driver to take us forward, regardless of what was in front of us.

We crushed the rear of the armoured car, and bulldozed it aside. The Panther reared up into the air as we lurched over the rubble of the collapsed house, through the phosphorous flames and into the street beyond.

Here, in the light of the flames, I could see some of our Volkssturm infantry, fighting with more Red soldiers who were firing from behind a wrecked T34. We bulldozed the Red panzer, pushing it aside and crushing some of the Russian infantry who were behind it. I saw that the survivors were set upon by our Volkssturm men, who knocked them down with carbine butts and even Panzerfausts which they wielded as clubs. As the Reds were subdued, hundreds of people began to surge forward again along the street, making for the far end. Behind us, the bombardment continued in its ferocious intensity.

I ordered the driver not to accelerate, as I could not bear the thought of crushed women and children under my tracks, however great the danger from the bombardment. As it was, the crowds were surging and scrambling away from the central part of the street, fighting each other to get into the smashed house fronts, into the side alleyways or even under the trees that lined the edges of the boulevard, to find any shelter from the explosions. Those that made it to the edges cowered there, squeezed against each other and transfixed in confusion, while those still in the middle of the street charged madly towards the far end where they knew the route to the West lay. Slowly, the space in front of us was cleared of people.

As the street emptied, we were able to pick up speed, and we travelled at about twenty kph for a short distance, aiming for the Western end which was framed between two high houses. I was still up out of the turret, with masonry and shrapnel whipping around me, and a few of our complement of riders was still crouched on our engine deck, clinging frantically to the grilles and equipment hooks. I thought that we were going to be successful, and reach the Western end - but without warning one of the King Tigers appeared in front of us, actually reversing backwards between the final houses into the main street again, his exhausts flaring. He came to a halt, traversing his turret, and began firing with his barrel below horizontal at something in the space beyond the street, which we could not see around the corner of the houses.

I had the feeling now that the Reds were playing with us – simply manoeuvring us around for their sport. They had allowed our column to enter and fill the narrow street, then started their bombardment just as our people were at their most exposed. Now they were blocking us off, sealing us in to this death channel, with most of our heavy panzers already out somewhere beyond the edge of the town.

Another artillery round exploded behind our Panther, and I heard screams from my rear deck as shrapnel cut into the people riding on our hull. Debris smashed off my cupola and hit me in the back, and I dropped down into the turret with stabs of pain shooting through my spine. I grabbed the 75mm gun breech for support, and the loader steadied me and unfastened my jacket to see the wound. Outside the Panther, metal was breaking in waves against our armour plate, and making our machine rock like a boat. The pain in my back prevented me from thinking about the effect of the explosions on the people taking cover in the street. At times, as the loader probed my back injury, I could hear long screams from outside, in the brief intervals between the explosions and the King Tiger firing his gun. I think that I also heard people beating and pounding on our armour, trying to climb aboard or calling desperately for help. At one moment, the open hatch of the cupola was filled with the hysterical, screaming face of a woman, begging to come into the panzer. I would have permitted her, but another shell exploded close to us, and she disappeared in a plume of smoke and debris.

Halbe was being systematically destroyed, I realised – from one end to the other end, second by second. I grunted as my loader removed the second of two shell splinters from my back, and then splashed antiseptic on the wound. I shuddered in pain, but was still grateful that I was inside the Panther, and not outside in the raging maelstrom of the street.

I gulped down an amphetamine tablet, and let the loader give me a short jab from a morphine capsule – enough to deaden the pain, but not enough to knock me out. I felt numb, wooden, and my limbs became distant from my body. I looked through the periscopes forward, and saw the King Tiger in front of us advancing slowly, surrounded by a mob of armed soldiers, civilians and others. There was a Kubelwagen (*VW jeep*) beside the rear of the panzer, and soldiers were fighting for space inside it, raining blows on each other. One man raised a pistol and shot an officer through the chest – and then the King Tiger jerked sideways as it accelerated, its massive tracks crushing the Kubelwagen, the officer and the mutinous soldier, destroying them and others under its treads.

With explosions blowing slabs of masonry off the walls of the houses around us, and entire buildings collapsing in bursts of smoke, we advanced behind the King Tiger out of the main street, being forced to drive over the crushed Kubelwagen and its shattered human debris as we progressed. Rounding the corner, I saw what the King Tiger had been firing at: a pair of T34 panzers were wedged between two buildings, their front hulls shot away and the bodies of their crews burning as they hung out of the hatches. Was that the Reds' last ambush, or were there more tricks still to come?

Around us, the ragged mass of our foot travellers scuttled and jumped alongside our Panther. This road had fewer opportunities for cover than the main street, being open on one side, but this allowed the people to spread out into the fields to the left in an attempt to avoid the exploding shells which were falling all around us. In all my experience in the East, I had not seen a bombardment this intense: shells landing one on top of the other, the dust cloud of one explosion being torn apart by the explosion of the next round, and among them the incendiary rockets crashing and exploding across the street and the open spaces.

Perhaps it was the amphetamine cocktail, but I grew immune to the sight of these rockets bursting among the hundreds of people who swarmed beside us, sending dozens of them tumbling in grotesque somersaults with their bodies on fire, their burning limbs carving patterns on my retina as they flailed in the dim light. A pair of horses pulling a cart were set on fire, and they stampeded insanely, throwing the civilians in the cart out behind them as they kicked and trampled on anyone unlucky enough to be in their path, until an artillery shell killed the animals in a puff of whirling flesh.

Several times we had to halt while the King Tiger in front of us dealt with threats that appeared from one side or another, its turret traversing and spitting tracer from its co-axial machine gun into the night. The great panzer had a group of SS troops on its back hull, and these men fired with MP40 and heavy machine guns into the houses as they saw enemy troops lurking in there.

We came on a partly collapsed building which had red troops firing from the rubble. An anti-tank rocket flew out from this strongpoint in a trail of fire and exploded against one of the huge concave wheels of the King Tiger. The wheel flew off, spinning like a coin, and for a moment I thought that the panzer was doomed. But the SS men leaped from the hull and stormed the Red position, throwing themselves onto the enemy guns. The surviving Reds swarmed out, firing their machine pistols into the mass of troops and civilians, running and swerving among the throng and shooting at random.

I pulled myself up through the hatch to see what was happening, and grabbed my machine pistol, climbing out onto the hull when I realised what was taking place. In the light of the burning buildings, I could see these ten or twelve Red troops – who knew they were about to die, but wanted to take as many Germans as possible with them – running madly through the ranks, shooting and yelling. Half of the Reds were felled in moments by shots or blows, and they disappeared under German boots as they were kicked and mauled to death. But others charged into a mass of civilians, shooting and cutting down women and children with sustained bursts of fire. One of these attackers was killed when an incendiary rocket landed near him, bounced into the air and decapitated him as he ran. His body ran on for several metres, still firing his gun, until it stumbled and fell.

I jumped off the Panther, feeling no pain from my wounds, and shot down two of the other Reds as they ran berserk among the fleeing civilians. Some of our troops came to my aid, shooting at the Reds and bringing them down – but many others, even those who had guns, were rooted to the ground with exhaustion or fear, and simply watched us as we, the more determined fighters, took on the enemy. In seconds, we had shot down all these Ivans, and the civilians were searching their bodies for food and pistols, even as the corpses steamed in the flickering light.

I clambered back onto the Panther, my body still numb, my mind clouded. We drove on down this exit street for fifty metres, then one hundred metres, away from the most intense area of bombardment. The artillery barrage slackened here, with the Red guns still focussing on the central part of the town, where a dreadful massacre must surely be taking place.

Looking back to the central area, I could make out a mass of people – not hundreds, but many thousands of them – crawling out from the street exit, dragging themselves away from the fire zone. Behind them, the buildings of central Halbe were completely aflame, and shells were still bursting over the houses with a frantic rhythm. What was the fate of the thousands who were still trying to break through back there, through the rockets and shell bursts in between the collapsed houses?

As if in answer to my question, a truck appeared in the exit from the main street: an open vehicle with a cab and a flat body. The body was loaded with troops and civilians, their bodies streaming with smoke and sparks. The truck was on fire, with flames erupting from its engine, and it careered out of control into the crowd in the open space, running down many people, who were then left where they fell. The truck rolled to a halt, and the flames around it grew and began to roar. I saw that none of the people on its body tried to move, dismount or climb off. Either too badly hurt, too terrified or too uncaring of their fate, they remained piled on the truck while it exploded into flames and the fire consumed them rapidly.

I looked ahead again, towards the darkness at the end of this road, a shadowy space not illuminated by flares, fires or explosions. Beside us, the survivors on foot herded forward, following the panzers towards their hope of safety. We slowed to walking pace, as I crouched on the turret top, communicating with my driver through the interphone, trying to make out what was ahead of us. I could not see the King Tigers, but I made out the exhausts of the Capo's Panther in the darkness, progressing slowly at an even pace. After several hundred metres, I noticed the people on the ground around us beginning to pick up speed, starting to run with their remaining energy towards the dark but silent area ahead. Motorcycles, trucks and horses streamed past us, dim shapes in the gloom, these vehicles and carts swerving among the foot traffic – all of us racing for the way out of Halbe.

'It seems that we are through, sir,' my gunner said in my earphones. 'There is nothing beyond. It looks like the road going West.'

I grunted a response – partly in doubt, partly because the pain of my back wound was starting to lever into my senses. My back was cool and wet – and I touched it to find it slick with blood. Perhaps when we were finally through, when we were crossing the land beyond Halbe, then I could find a medic and have the wounds dressed.

'I really think we're through,' my driver said from his position down in the front hull. 'I can see a sign ahead. What does it say, sir?'

I peered into the dark, my vision doubling as if I was drunk. There *was* a sign there: some kind of placard on a roadside tree, white with black letters, and as we approached I saw that it was a hand-painted route marker.

All German traffic, progress right
The secure route is through the railroad station
By Order
Reich Field Police

I told the driver to rotate right, and to advance slowly towards the station. The mass of people around us swarmed together, reading the sign, shouting out in hopes of deliverance, believing they were almost out of the Kessel.

After a hundred metres, we passed a solitary German soldier, in a clean, tidy uniform, a man who appeared well-fed and healthy. I was so accustomed to the sight of our ragged, patched-up infantry that I noted this immediately, even in the moonlight and in my drugged state. He directed us to the right, using a field police direction pointer, and he saluted professionally. I did not have time to note his insignia – and anyway, the light was getting too dim. Following his directions, we progressed right – and in a few moments I saw the iron foot bridge of the railway station in front of us under the moon. More of these clean, professional German soldiers appeared beside the road, waving us forward and pointing to the station area.

'We're through,' my driver said. 'See these field police fellows? They must have come up from the Twelfth Army Zone. We'll be linking up soon, sir, won't we?'

'If they're the Twelfth Army, they're too far forward,' my gunner said. 'They should be thirty kilometres to the West.'

I nodded at his comment, looking at another of the field police in his smartly pressed uniform, as he waved us on to the station zone. I suddenly shouted to my driver to halt, and the Panther ground to a stop in a swirl of dust and earth. The foot traffic did not halt, but surged around us, a multitude of troops, civilians and wheeled transports following the police directions to the station. Even the troops clinging to our rear deck jumped off, now that we were halted, and joined the crowd surging forward along the road. I looked down at the field policeman, his eyes invisible under the rim of his helmet, and his uniform devoid of insignia.

'What unit are you with?' I called to him, over the noise of explosions from the town and the tramping of the foot soldiers charging past towards the station.

'Field police, Herr Feldwebel,' the man saluted.

I climbed down from the Panther slowly, with pain rippling through my spine, and stood in front of him. The hundreds of foot soldiers and civilians charged around us, shouting encouragement to each other.

'Which unit of field police?' I asked the man, over the heads of the people rushing between us.

'You must hurry, Herr Feldwebel,' he called to me. 'The Reds are close.'

'Which unit of police?' I shouted, being rocked and jostled by the many troops rushing past. A civilian woman passed between us, dragging a child in each hand – children of five or six years, trailing their feet in exhaustion.

'The rail station,' she was saying. 'We will be safer there.'

'Which unit are you with?' I shouted to the field police soldier. 'Which unit?'

He was gone.

He had retreated into the shadows away from the road, and I caught sight of his back as he ducked between trees in the pasture, dodging away from us.

'*Seydlitz truppe,*' I yelled. 'These are Seydlitz men!'

The Seydlitz men were a curse on us all.

Seydlitz troops were German soldiers who had surrendered to the Reds in the East, and had agreed to work for them to disrupt our lines and cause confusion. I had heard of them often – but never seen one until now. They were notorious for exactly this – wearing German uniforms, they planted false signposts, directed traffic wrongly, and fouled up the plans of entire regiments.

Hundreds of people began breaking and running past our panzer towards the station. I could see them, converging in the moonlight on the access road, running, limping, dragging themselves towards what they thought was safety.

'These are Seydlitz men!' I shouted to the onrushing troops, trying to push them back. Several of them halted, and a knot of troops and civilians gathered around me, but the vast bulk of this tide of people surged on past us. I shouted to them to stop, to stay away from the station, to ignore the signs.

Inside the station, the shooting began within seconds.

I saw the muzzle flashes light up the footbridge in the darkness, not only from one side, but from both ends of the site. Screams tore the air among the rapid, unceasing machine gun shots, and the crowd surging to the station faltered, stumbled, and many fell. The people behind them, though, were confused and running blindly, not seeing where the shots were coming from, and they kept rushing on, trampling and stamping on those who were falling. Within seconds, in addition to the massacre taking place inside the station, the ground around our panzer was strewn with wounded and trampled foot soldiers, civilians and children, as the crowd broke and began to run wildly for any available cover.

I leaped back onto the Panther and ordered the driver to advance on the station. That was hopeless, though – the entrance area was thick with people, especially civilians with carts, huddling together and not knowing which way to turn. The shooting from the station reached a crescendo, and grenades began to explode in there, with the characteristic hollow crack of the Soviet bombs that spread such vicious splinters. The dim landscape was lit by these flashes, and by the shouts and screams of the trapped victims from within the station precincts, and still by the fires and detonations of the bombardment in Halbe itself.

A soldier came running out of the station, his face a mask of blood, his eyes wide and staring.

'Make the people follow you,' he shouted to me. 'They will follow a panzer, Herr Feldwebel. Lead them away from the station, for God's sake.'

'But the people in the station - '

'They are dead, all dead,' he shouted. 'Lead these others away, in the name of God!'

We drove the Panther slowly away from the station, across the open ground, scattering the milling crowds of leaderless, confused soldiers and frantic civilians. They formed up behind us, in the constant manner of stragglers, and stumbled after us as we moved away. I dreaded encountering land mines in this open space, or a return of the intense artillery bombardment, but we entered a heathland punctuated by bracken and scrub, in which, with only the moonlight and distant flames, it was difficult to make out any way ahead.

A civilian man who knew the area climbed up beside me, and with his directions we crawled away from Halbe, picking up a narrow road that crossed the Halbe rail line at a barrier point. This crossing was strewn with abandoned trucks and equipment, and beyond it the road led west through overhanging trees, going into a forest. There were flashes here as artillery shells exploded in the fields on either side, but these were fired randomly and caused only limited casualties to the massed ranks behind us. It became too dark to navigate, or to steer, and the danger of shedding a track or grounding the Panther and damaging its running gear was a constant anxiety. A shape loomed up in front of us, with two red, glowing stacks – and we almost collided with the Capo's Panther which was stationary at a curve in the forest track. We took the decision to halt and move on at first light.

A few minutes later, at around two in the morning, our two Panthers were concealed under trees off the road, and the horde of

infantry and others who had followed us away from the station were
finding places to lay themselves down on the pine needles between
the tree trunks. From among the infantry, we posted a perimeter
guard, and then we broke into a forestry hut that our civilian guide
found for us. Inside, in the dark, the Capo said,

'So we are through Halbe. The King Tigers are somewhere
ahead now, we have simply lost touch with them. We must carry on
by ourselves for now. We have to watch out for those Seydlitz men.
I hear that the station was packed with dead bodies, three or four
deep.'

'We can identify the Seydlitz men by their uniforms,' I said.
'They are clean and well presented. Unlike our troops.'

The Capo peered through the window shutter at the crowds of
troops and civilians outside.

'Our troops know that the war is lost,' he said. 'How many want
to fight now? Only a quarter or a third of our men will fight any
longer. The rest will let others fight for them.'

'Then we will fight with the quarter or the third,' I said.

The Capo lit a kerosene lamp on minimum light, and unfolded
a map.

'I took this from a dead artillery man,' he said. 'See here, it
shows where we are.'

He showed me our location. We were in a triangular stretch of
woodland, South West of Halbe, which was bisected by the country
railroad and by various forestry tracks. The map extended West to
the Elbe itself, where the Twelfth Army were holding open the corridor that would lead us to the Americans. Between our patch of
forest and the Twelfth Army were two remaining milestones to cross.

First, the North-South Autobahn that ran up and down this part
of Germany, dead straight. We believed that the Russians had just
charged up this Autobahn in their advance on Berlin itself to the
North. If so, most of their forces would be fighting in Berlin, leaving
the rural hinterland thinly guarded.

'That's the plan,' the Capo said. 'And after we cross the Autobahn,
we have to cross the railroad line, about twenty kilometres further.

After that, we should find the Twelfth Army boys waiting for us. And then, hello America.'

His finger moved across the map. The Autobahn, the railroad, and then the River Elbe. I laughed in a grim way, but that only made the pain in my back sharper.

—

In the past, I had slept easily enough in a panzer: the thin, metal chair made a good perch, and you rested your head on the turret wall or on the gun breech, with your forehead on your linked fingers for a pillow. If you were in the panzer all night, a shell case was your toilet, and fresh air came from opening the hatch to empty it. In this way, three men could pass the night in the turret cage, and the other two crew men on their seats in the hull.

On that night in the woodland West of Halbe, though, I did not want to sleep. I took another mouthful of amphetamines, painkillers and schnapps. The forest around my Panther was not sleeping either: it was filled with voices, cries, the wailing of children and the sound of equipment being readied for our next stage of the breakout. Searching for aspirin, I fumbled in my tunic pocket, and found the photo of the young woman that the lady on the Panther's deck had given me before she died. A grey light was coming through the cupola, and I climbed out to examine the photo more fully. The girl was a beauty, and like all lonely soldiers, I imagined that she might be good, understanding company for a man such as me. There was an address on the back, a town to the west of the Elbe, in the American occupied sector of Germany. There was no name for the girl. I smiled, and put the photo safely in my pocket again.

A few birds were singing, but that stopped as the sound of bombardment grew from the countryside to our West. Close at hand, in the forest, there was more noise – shouting and cursing, and people clamouring for attention.

I went into the trees to see what this was. I found a scrum of our soldiers hunched over something on the ground, in the dawn light.

I pushed through them, and with the authority that came from a panzer uniform at this point in the fighting, the infantry made way for me slowly. I found that a group of German troops had found a Seydlitz man.

The Seydlitz agent was pressed back against the roots of a tree, clenching his fists, gritting his teeth. His field-grey uniform had a German eagle but no swastika, and one of our men handed me an armband that had been in the Seydlitz man's pocket.

In the service of The National Committee for a Free Germany

This was what the Seydlitz agents called their organisation. Looking around, I realised that the small crowd did not only contain soldiers. Various German women were present, some of them armed, and also a handful of children and youths of about ten years to maybe fifteen years of age. One of the women stepped forward, and threw a rope upward, over the branch of the nearest tree.

An aircraft flew overhead, then another two planes, so low that their slipstream shook the tree canopy. I heard their cannon firing into the forest to the East, and then the slow thump of exploding vehicles from somewhere over there.

With this background, the Seydlitz man was hanged on the tree, his throat emitting a dreadful rattle, while the circle of troops, youths and women watched. His jerking, kicking heels were seized by a German boy of ten or twelve years, who swung and pulled on them to break the Seydlitz man's neck and silence the hideous sounds that were coming from his mouth.

'It is not decent,' I heard the boy say to his mother, as the hanged man's feet swung around silently in a circle above us. 'Such sounds are not decent in a German forest.'

—

THE AUTOBAHN AND THE RAILROAD

We moved slowly out to the main path, which was already filling up with mismatched human and vehicle traffic that had entered this patch of forest during darkness, having traversed the nightmare of Halbe itself. We set our compass and aimed West. I moved ahead of the Capo's Panther, and together our two panzers advanced at walking pace, with frequent stops, in the pearlescent light of the spring morning. On our left, incendiary explosions rolled across the horizon, and from the Panther's cupola I could see trees in the distant fields being blown up and set on fire by the blasts. I believed that the unit there were the remains of our 21st Division Panzergrenadiers, holding back the Reds from our columns. At times, wounded infantry would appear in the pastures near the road, limping or carrying their comrades. They told us that the line was holding over there, but the Reds were constantly probing our flanks with their panzers, infantry and Seydlitz men.

The Sturmoviks came over us repeatedly, so often that the air was almost never free of the scream of their engines. There was a Flak gun on a broken-down half- track at one point in a copse near the road, manned by a crew of Hitler Youth, Luftwaffe men and civilian girls. This ragged crew threw off their camouflage netting and foliage, and fired up at the swooping Red aircraft. They managed to hit one plane – sending tracer through one wing, and causing a huge plume of flame to erupt from it. The Sturmovik flipped onto its back, with metal debris streaming out in the flames in its slipstream, and crashed into the forest ahead. The victory was momentary: the following two planes spotted the Flak at once, and raked it with their incendiary shells, leaving the bodies of the crew burning among the barrels of their gun.

In the early light, the Russian forces tested us and pushed at our lines. Our two Panthers were moving with a group of about five hundred infantry and civilians who had come through Halbe with us, and we were in no condition to withstand a sustained attack from the flanks. As the sun rose, my worst fears in this respect became a reality.

Through the trees, we saw that three Josef Stalin panzers had appeared outside the forest, on the distant heath, patrolling across the open land and traversing their turrets as they surveyed our segment of the woodland. We immediately halted, trusting that our vehicles were screened by the trees, and we watched the Stalins as they prowled across the landscape out there. To engage them would surely bring a further detachment of Red panzers down upon us, leading to the destruction of the few hundred people we had brought through from Halbe. Our column of foot soldiers and civilians, meanwhile, threw themselves onto the forest floor, and drove their animals off among the trees.

In moments, our thousand pairs of eyes were watching silently as the three Stalins moved slowly past our part of the treeline, at a distance of about one kilometre from us.

I was inside the turret, and my gunner had his face to the gun sight, with his hand on the firing lever, his feet moving the turret fractionally to keep the Stalins in his scope. I could see the sweat dripping down the side of his neck, and the quiver in his fingers as he held the lever.

For a panzer commander, one immediate tactical decision in a concealment situation is whether to shut down your vehicle's engine or not. The engine, even when idling, is noisy; and if the enemy for some reason shuts off *his* engine, he will hear you; or, if the enemy is accompanied by an infantry screen, they will hear you if they move away from the sound of their own panzers. On the other hand, if you turn your engine off, there is the danger that it may be slow to start if you need to move away urgently, and also, without the transmission running under the turret, you can only traverse your turret slowly with the hand crank. Weighing this up, I kept the engine running – because the enemy Stalins were still some distance away, and I could see no infantry with them.

As another precaution, I ordered my loader to load high explosive and have a round of armor-piercing ready in his hands. Like the T34s against the King Tigers, I knew that the best way to deal with a bigger, heavier tank was to blow its tracks off with the first shot, and then to use a penetrating round. The three Stalins came closer, and then halted, trailing fumes, at a range of barely six to eight hundred metres outside the trees.

I swallowed.

The Stalins spewed out exhaust smoke, and then continued their slow progress past us. Five hundred hearts were pounding in rhythm with their engines, I am sure. As they began to depart, the rearmost Stalin turned its turret to us, and fired a long burst of machine gun from its co-axial along our tree line. The bullets ripped up the trees at head height, and ricocheted off the hull of our Panther, and then ceased. Apparently satisfied, the Stalin moved on slowly.

I breathed in deep relief – but as I did so, a civilian man bolted out from the trees beside us, waving his arms in surrender.

'*Scheisse*, he's gone mad under the pressure,' my radio man said.

The civilian was an elderly man, and he was followed by two more people – a woman and a girl, who were either seeking to surrender also, or trying to restrain their relative before he gave us all away. I then saw a Wehrmacht soldier near my panzer stand up, aim with his carbine and shoot the three people down, one after the other. They tumbled and fell like rabbits in the long grass. I had no time for sympathy – I was watching that last Stalin. The great panzer halted, and rotated its hull to face onto us.

'He saw the shooting,' my driver said. 'Or he saw the people running.'

Our luck was that bad – that the Stalin commander had seen the civilians run and fall, and he wanted to know why. The Stalin fired a shot: a high explosive round which burst in the trees above and sent shrapnel and wood blasting down around us. A group of civilians was hit, and they began charging in panic out onto the heath. Several soldiers also went out, with their hands raised. They were immediately cut down by the Stalin's machine gun, which swept across them at neck height, decapitating many of the men. Their headless bodies slumped down, with their hands still raised. The other two Stalins turned front-on to us, and began firing their main guns into the woods also.

The rounds tore open the tree line in front of us, and despite the smoke, the many people running and hiding on the edge of the forest must now have become visible. A tree crashed to earth, revealing our Panther fully. In some ways, I was relieved – now we were to fight as panzer men again, machine against machine, and not hide with the old men and the fearful women in the forest. I ordered my gunner to fire the high explosive round in the breech.

Our round was laid perfectly, and it exploded just right of centre against the front plate of that Stalin which had discovered us. Through the periscope, I saw its drive wheel go spinning away, dragging the track with it. The Stalin's barrel was still lowered for its lengthy reloading, and for these few moments the Red panzer was vulnerable.

We fired again, with the armour-piercing, and this shot struck the Stalin on the gun mantle. I saw the whole turret jerk with the concussion, as metal debris flew around the machine. The Stalin began trying to reverse, keeping its front facing to us, but its missing track meant that it moved slowly, and was dragging itself at an angle. If that Red driver panicked now, and accelerated, the single track would slew the whole vehicle sideways and present its thinner flank armour to us. I ordered my gunner to hold fire unless this happened. Meanwhile, we advanced out of the trees, onto the flat land, to engage the enemy with freedom of movement.

To my right, the Capo's Panther was firing on the other two Stalins, his tracer rebounding off one of them, hitting the other and deflecting from that one off into the heathland. The Capo too moved out onto the heath, halting to aim his next shot. A round from one of the Stalins hit his turret top and ricocheted off, carving a path through the trees between us. I saw that a group of our infantry were approaching those two Stalins from the side, with Panzerfausts, and it appeared the Russian crews had not seen them.

I heard my gunner grunt in anticipation – and saw that the disabled Stalin had begun to speed up, the movement turning its flank towards us. The Stalin twitched as the single track gripped the ground, and in a spray of dust it began to turn sideways on, with its big silhouette clear in the morning haze. My gunner put his shot cleanly through the lower hull, just above the running gear. For a moment, the Stalin kept moving, as if the round had not penetrated – but then the turret began to traverse wildly and the whole machine began to shudder. I knew what was happening in there: the exploding ammunition in the hull was building up a blast wave of pressure which would inevitably rip the turret from the hull, or split the hull itself open. No panzer ever built could withstand such internal pressures. Indeed, the Stalin's long, oblong turret suddenly rose up into the air, lifted by a flash of expanding flame, and tumbled over, spilling out the bodies of the turret crew. The hull lay juddering, sending out spirals of exploding ammunition into the morning light.

Both our Panthers focussed now on the two remaining Stalins. Those Red gun barrels were elevated again, and from the traversing of their turrets I saw that they were both taking aim at my Panther. I told my driver to accelerate, out into the heath, hoping that we could move faster than their turrets could turn. At the same time, we traversed our turret rapidly onto them, finishing our short run with a slew to one side, to bring our gun more quickly around to aim at the Reds. A few seconds of shouted commands, my gunner rotating the turret a few centimetres and operating the gun elevation for his final calculations. Just as the Stalins turned their massive guns directly onto us, my gunner was able to get a shot onto the nearest one, a shot which at this close range split open the top of the turret where it joined the side.

I saw the projectile exit the turret through the hatch, carrying with it parts of the crews' bodies and bits of machinery. The open hatch emitted thick smoke, and the lower hull crew began to clamber out.

The other Stalin, before it could get a shot at us, was hit by a Panzerfaust. I saw our men advancing to the machine's rear, ducking as they scrambled across the scrubland from the woods. I saw the long, fiery trail of a Panzerfaust rocket, and then the explosion from the engine compartment which sent a torrent of fuel spilling out onto the heath. That crew also climbed out of their panzer, and in a few seconds our men had rounded up half a dozen of these Russian crew men, standing around them with their guns trained on them while our two Panthers drove back to the road through the forest. We had won this small battle against great odds – but the smoke from the burning Stalins was marking our position clearly even in the morning mist, and for every Stalin that we destroyed, five could come to take its place.

As we regained the road, with the Capo's panzer in front, I saw that our infantry were shooting the captured Red crewmen, cutting them down one by one with single rounds. Then our men searched the bodies, removing what appeared to be cigarettes and items of food. Our troops had descended this low: scavenging scraps from enemy corpses.

I told my driver to make the fastest possible speed on this narrow, uneven road. It was imperative that we get away from that scene urgently. I went up through the hatch and looked around. The five hundred or so infantry and civilians were forming up behind us, hobbling, limping or walking in our wake. If I expected congratulations on our rapid battle, none were forthcoming: the wounded were in their own world, and the civilians were ashen-faced and trembling. The mist overhead began to burn off in the sunlight. In a few minutes, the bombing began again, with Sturmoviks passing overhead and dropping bombs at random through the leaf cover.

I stood on the rear deck, as wounded men and exhausted civilians began to drag themselves up on board, and I considered the state of the Panther. We had fuel for another twenty kilometres at best. The transmission was almost worn out. The engine was running hot, and the tracks needed to be removed, tightened and their connecting pins checked – a procedure that would take half a day under normal circumstances. Our main gun ammunition was down to a handful of rounds, with almost none left for the machine guns. Our radio had stopped functioning properly, and we had no fire extinguisher or spare oil. The superb, slab-sided Panther kept rolling West at a walking pace, but for how much longer?

This road passed through an area where the Russians had fought running battles with our forces in the days before. The forest was strewn with wrecked vehicles, both German and Russian. We passed a series of German ambulance vans, in which each of the wounded men had been shot in the head. The discovery gave renewed impetus to our column's march, as our two panzers and then the infantry and foot followers filed past the human remains, even as our loader jumped down to tap the vans for any possible fuel.

We stopped at any intact vehicles that we found, to check them for fuel in the tanks, but somebody had been through the area ahead of us and drained every drop. There was a T34 still in one piece, surrounded by the bodies of its crew – but the Russian panzers ran on diesel, not gasoline, and that fuel would cause our Maybach engines to foul up. The need for gasoline was becoming desperate, and preying on my mind as much as the explosions from aircraft and artillery which echoed around us.

Around midday, in a clearing which was untouched by the battles, we came upon a remarkable thing.

It was a Panther.

The panzer was stationary, halted among the ferns, apparently undamaged. It appeared to be virtually new, its paint unchipped and its tracks perfectly tensioned, with no mud or debris in them. Its hatches were closed, and its gun was level.

We halted and observed it for a minute. There was no sign of life. I walked across to the Capo's panzer, climbed up among his wounded and discussed this with him.

'No markings or signs,' the Capo said, squinting at the beautiful, unmarked Panther in the dappled light. 'It's just been abandoned, perhaps. Maybe it ran out of fuel. But then why did the crew not blow it up with the demolition charge?'

'Maybe the crew surrendered or were killed outside the vehicle,' I said. 'It could be full of gasoline. And ammunition. It might start at the first try.'

The Capo looked at me.

'You suggest leaving your Panther and taking that Panther?'

'Or putting our radio man in that one. He can drive well enough, and he has no radio or gun ammunition anyway. We can pick up more panzer crew men along the road. Then we will have a force of three Panthers.'

The Capo rubbed his chin.

'But who would leave a panzer there like that? It looks like a Red trick to me. As if they captured a Panther and then left it here as a trap.'

'Let me take a look, Herr Leutnant.'

'Be very quick. And be careful.'

I went over to the Panther and looked around it. I could see no cables or trip wires, and the ground appeared undisturbed. The machine looked the way that my machine used to: pristine, well-maintained, and very potent. I climbed up onto it and tried the commander's hatch. It slid to one side easily. I waited for a few seconds.

There was an explosion which sent a torrent of fire up into the air, to a height of twenty metres. I could hear debris flying around inside the panzer, as its ammunition detonated, and then, as I jumped clear and ran, the fuel tanks blew up with a force that suggested they had been completely full. I stumbled, as a fireball rose over the Panther, and it was covered in burning gasoline. As I picked myself up, the Capo laughed and ordered us to move on quickly.

'You thought it was Christmas morning, Faust,' he shouted at me. 'You thought the Reds gave you a new Panther. But the Reds know how to set a trap, that's for sure.'

We left the magnificent Panther burning there, as the trees around it caught fire, and the Sturmovik aircraft overhead began to swarm towards the smoke.

—

In the late afternoon, our road converged with several other tracks in an area of oak trees dotted with small houses inside the forest. The narrow roads were crammed with traffic and people, all heading West towards the North-South Autobahn. Basic military discipline had broken down in this area. There was nobody directing the traffic, and panzers, half-tracks, motorcycle combinations and cars all scraped alongside each other as the final, single road had to take all of the vehicles and people. The forest was dense overhead, but to either side was more open country, and we could hear the sound of fighting from left and right as the troops on the flanks fought to keep the narrow route open.

I began to see, among the roadside bushes, small shapes that fluttered in the breeze and trailed long threads. These were the epaulettes, shoulder badges and collar insignia of officers and NCOs, who did not want to be captured with the enemy knowing their rank, and they had torn their markings off and thrown them away. Almost all of these were the badges of regular Wehrmacht or Luftwaffe troops, gleaming dully in the light. I saw a few SS markings strewn by the roadside too: the skull badge or the collar flashes that would identify them as the Russian's worst enemies. However, most SS men were identifiable by their high-quality camouflage uniforms, or by their forearm tattoos which contained their blood group. For the SS, the only choice was to get to the West. The alternative was simply death. For years, they had sown destruction in the East, and now the enemy had them in an iron claw.

Slowly, we made our way towards the Western edge of the forest, and the great Autobahn road beyond. We managed to take some gasoline from a stranded truck full of Luftwaffe officer cadets, and we had to hold these boys back at gunpoint while we poured their cans of fuel into our panzers to gain another ten kilometres of movement. This was the law of the Kessel: he who could take what he needed, had to take it. The Luftwaffe cadets stood cursing and swearing vengeance on us as we left them behind.

As we approached the edge of the trees, a rocket bombardment began to smash into the rear of our column. The Katyusha rockets tore down through the oaks, smacking from one great trunk to another, setting the branches on fire and raining a burning liquid down onto the people there. It was essential that we leave this forest, or everyone here would be consumed within hours.

From the front of the column, an SS panzer man came running beside the road, calling for all panzers or armour to move to the front. Behind him, a squad of SS infantry were moving along the road, pushing all unarmoured vehicles or foot traffic to one side to let the panzers through. The Capo's Panther and mine made our way forward in answer to the call, crushing cars or carts which had not been moved aside. We even had to bulldoze aside a complete 88mm gun, which was stuck on its trailer in a crater, blocking the path.

Behind us, from out of the smoke of the burning trees, there appeared a convoy of Hetzers – the little self-propelled tracked guns that were fast and low, lightly armoured but useful to have in any situation. It was amazing to think that the complete Hetzer vehicle, at barely sixteen tonnes, weighed less than the turret on a King Tiger, which I believe weighed eighteen tonnes. How many more Hetzers could Germany have built, for the cost of the five hundred King Tigers which we produced in total in our factories? Two thousand Hetzers, or three thousand? What effect would this have had on the war? Such questions can lead to all manner of calculations and alternatives.

We were joined also by a Panzer IV of a tank training regiment, crewed by youths led by an experienced NCO, who stood in his turret hatch in an old-style black panzer tunic as if he was rolling into Poland at the start of this whole war. With this clutch of vehicles, we moved up to the head of the column, and dispersed among dense trees along the edge of an old gravel quarry.

The quarry was full of wounded, who were set out on the ground among the stones, and these men called to us pitifully not to leave them behind. I turned my head away and tried to shut out the sounds, as we panzer crews assembled with the SS men and moved quickly to the edge of the forest itself.

Three King Tigers were concealed here, their massive outlines shrouded in nets and branches. These were not the vehicles we had come through Halbe with, but from the 10th SS Panzers, which was reduced to this number as its entire strength. The unit was commanded by a Waffen SS Major with a bandage around his head and burn marks on his face. The SS had grim, clenched faces – as befitted men who were seeking to escape certain death at the hands of their captors – and their dilated, darkened eyes suggested that they were drawing strength from their supplies of cognac and amphetamine.

The SS had set up a binocular periscope here, and through it we could survey the edge of the woods, a short stretch of land, and then a dark ribbon cutting through the landscape from north to south.

'That is the Autobahn,' the SS Major said. 'Beyond that there is the railroad, and then the Twelfth Army.'

'Where are the Reds?' the Capo asked him. 'There is less bombardment out there in the open.'

'I think the Reds are waiting,' the SS man said. 'They came up this road on their way to Berlin three days ago. Almost all their forces are centred there to the North, but they must expect we will break out somewhere here. We captured a Red officer this morning who told us that they are bringing more armoured units down the Autobahn from Berlin tonight. They plan to fortify the Autobahn and make sure that nobody can cross it. See, the Autobahn goes through a cutting which would be perfect to defend. If the Reds build up in strength there, we will never get past this point.'

'Where is this prisoner?' the Capo asked.

'He is dead now. The information is accurate, we made sure of that.' The SS man lit a cigarette. He grinned suddenly. 'American cigarettes,' he explained. 'I have a contact who acquired a whole truckload in the Ardennes. Here, have one. Everybody have one.'

A Red Jabo flew over the tree line, firing rockets to the right of us. Nevertheless, we all took a cigarette, and inhaled the smoke. The tobacco was fresh, and fragrant, in a way that I remembered from my first cigarette before the war. It was rich and...what was the word?

'Quality,' one of the Hetzer men said. 'This is quality tobacco.'

'This is what life is like under the Americans,' the SS Major said. 'And the Americans will need men such as us to rebuild this country. I don't know about you, but I can speak some English.' He did not flinch as more Red planes screamed overhead, firing cannon through the trees. Empty cannon shell cases from these planes fell through the branches and landed around us.

'What is the plan for crossing the Autobahn?' the Panzer IV man asked. 'I assume that with your heavy panzers, you will be in the lead.'

'Yes,' the Major nodded, looking us all in the eye. 'We will cross at dusk. My three King Tigers will go out and cross first. We will hold open the way for the columns behind us,' he gestured with his cigarette into the forest, 'for all these columns to cross the Autobahn. But we also need screening panzers to move north and south of the crossing point. Those panzers will prevent enemy armour from approaching and disrupting the crossing. I want the three Hetzers and one Panther to the South, and the Panzer IV and the other Panther to the north, each grouped along the Autobahn cutting. My SS Panzergrenadiers will accompany you, and there are still infantry units in the columns who will fight. Some of the civilians are well armed now, so they can be useful to us as well. In this way, we will open the crossing, and in darkness our whole columns can cross at speed. After that, we must drive West without stopping. I repeat, we will not stop. You must keep up, or be left behind for the Russians.' He grinned suddenly. 'And then I will see you on the Elbe. We will be prisoners, but we will have plenty of cigarettes, my friends.'

—

The Capo stood on the edge of the gravel quarry, staring down at the doomed wounded on their grimy blankets: men who knew they were being abandoned.

'Two more battles,' he said. 'The Autobahn and then the rail line. For me, there is no choice in the matter. I must not be taken prisoner by the Reds. My family are in the West, and any future that I have is in the West. I cannot do ten or twenty years in a Soviet prison in Siberia. I cannot do it.'

'And if we are wounded?'

'That is a risk I shall take. Look, Faust. If you want to stay back. If you want to surrender, or cross the Autobahn with the column behind us, that is understandable. The war is almost over, and I cannot force you to fight. See here – look at all this.'

He pointed to a tree on the edge of the quarry. A large number of German insignia had been thrown here, hundreds of epaulettes and collars, dangling in the breeze. Among them, were many German tunic badges of the eagle with the swastika; the broad, silver wings of the eagle were fluttering idly among the leaves, trailing their ripped-off threads, the myriad swastikas discarded like omens of bad luck.

'You see, it is over,' the Capo said. 'But my life must not be over. For the sake of my children. For you, Faust, perhaps it is different. You have no family, do you?'

I took from my pocket the crumpled photograph of the unknown girl that had been with me from my first day in the Kessel, and showed it to him.

'I will come with you to the West,' I said.

'You're a strange fellow, Faust. You're half killer and half romantic.'

'Thank you, sir.'

I took an amphetamine tablet and swallowed it down with a gulp of schnapps, and finally squeezed the last of an ampoule of morphine into my mouth and swallowed that. I waited a few seconds for the combined effect to hit me. I jumped onto the turret as if I was weightless, and took command of the Panther through the headphones. In the side of my vision, I could see the massed ranks of the abandoned wounded lying in the quarry floor, and I forced myself not to look at them. The headphones on my ears blocked out, partly, the sound of their cries. Before my engine started, I heard, nevertheless, a series of single shots, the impacts coming one after the other at irregular intervals.

I could not stop myself looking back.

Some of the wounded troops were committing suicide. A pistol was passing from one hand to another, being fumbled among the blood-stained clothing. The men's desperate, open mouths sought the muzzle of the gun, like so many helpless chicks seeking their food.

—

I was to seal off the southern Autobahn with the three Hetzers and a mobile Flak on a Famo half-track, which had a quadruple 20mm cannon. This was quite a strong group of vehicles for such a task, and we were accompanied by two Hanomags of SS Panzergrenadiers who would act to secure the crossing, and then be replaced by Wehrmacht as the SS moved West. All in all, this was a respectable battle group, and I felt confident that we could hold the crossing open in the early stages, provided that more armour came up from inside the Kessel as the night progressed.

We moved out towards the Autobahn as the sun set. The Western sky, towards which we were striving with such hope, was streaked with red. The land around the road was scattered with the debris of the Russians' advance North to Berlin, which had cleaved our forces in two and sealed the Kessel from the West in the preceding days. A ruined T34 and a Panzer IV were jammed together, burned out and wrecked. A Luftwaffe reconnaissance aircraft lay on its back, its two pilots dead in the glass cabin. Shell craters were filled with the bodies of Soviets, Wehrmacht and civilians, their jumbled faces staring up with a waxen pallor.

As soon as our tracks bit into the dry ground here and threw up dust, an aircraft appeared in the sky overhead. This was a Russian 'Lame Duck' type, the little biplanes used for spotting and nuisance bombing. Our Flak vehicle drove it away with bursts of tracer which spiralled up luminously in the grey light – but not before the plane had dropped a white parachute flare marking our location.

In this sinister glow, I saluted the Capo, as his Panther and the old Panzer IV moved off to guard the Northern flank of the crossing point, while I moved South with the Hetzers.

As soon as we approached the Autobahn itself, we came under fire from the far side. A red tracer round flashed from a clump of trees and hit the Hetzer which was next to me. The range was less than a kilometre, and the force of the round lifted the whole top of the Hetzer's body from the hull, sending it up into the air in front of me. The little vehicle caught fire immediately, and continued rolling forward for some distance, with its crew burning within the open hull. My gunner responded to the attack with a high explosive round which blew aside some of the trees where the enemy was located. I could make out a huge, block-shaped machine, equipped with a massive gun: an SU tank destroyer. These colossal machines were nothing more than mobile steel fortresses, but their battleship guns could be fatal to any panzer in their path.

To my North, the two SS King Tigers broached the Autobahn and came to a halt straddling the black road and its lines of wreckage. They engaged the SU at a range of about 1.5 kilometres, firing together across the plain. In moments, the SU was hit with a strike that knocked its massive gun mantle off to one side, and smoke began to coil from its hull.

With the two remaining Hetzers, my Panther too came onto the Autobahn, and we positioned ourselves along it with the Panther on the left and the two surviving Hetzers staggered on the right. Our two Hanomags of SS men leaped from their transports and took up positions beside the road, with heavy machine guns and Panzerfausts. Dusk was gathering, but overhead the drifting parachute flare cast a light similar to dawn; fortunately, a strong breeze was carrying it away from us, to the South West.

I surveyed the long, straight Autobahn through the cupola periscopes, trusting to the King Tigers on my right to guard our rear as they broke through the Red lines. The landscape was being lit by flashes and bursts of fire as they engaged the armour they were encountering. I took a quick look in that direction – and, with the drugs affecting my mind, I was transfixed at what I saw.

On the great, open plain, one King Tiger stood out in the glow of dusk, silhouetted against the skyline. It was immobilised, with its massive tracks twisted around, and one drive wheel lying beside it. Unmoving, though, it continued to fire as its comrade Tiger moved ahead, covering the other Tiger against a group of SU destroyers which were approaching. The immobile Tiger crew seemed determined to use all their ammunition, and were shooting at a rapid pace, again and again, each shot illuminating the huge, doomed machine.

I saw one of its rounds streak across the plain and blow the hatches off one of the SU machines. The Red destroyer emitted a pall of smoke, and tipped into a crater, spinning around to expose its flank. The Tiger pierced it through the side with another round, which exited upward through the engine grilles and rose perhaps a hundred metres into the air, the tracer still glowing. The crew of that SU began to clamber out, but they were caught by a horizontal burst from one of our Flak half-tracks, cutting them to pieces where they stood.

The King Tiger engaged in a death duel with the two remaining SU guns. The Reds slowly shot the great panzer to pieces, one round knocking off its running gear, and causing the wheels to spin wildly over the ground. Another shell exploded on the turret, sending the cupola off into the air. Still the King Tiger kept firing, as its comrade panzer pushed forward to the west, shooting up the resistance that it was encountering there. The stricken Tiger, wreathed in smoke and with its wheels and tracks destroyed, fired on, immobilising one of the SUs by exploding a high explosive shell low on its front plate. I could see the SU's drive wheels spinning, but the tracks were separated and it was unable to move.

The other destroyer shot up our King Tiger with slow, repeated rounds: one that hit the front plate and deflected off, then another which hit the gun mantle and deflected down onto the hull in a puff of metal fragments. The SU prowled to the flank of the Tiger, even as our panzer sought to traverse its turret onto the enemy. Two final shots blew off the Tiger's engine covers, sending burning gasoline over the hull, and then punched a hole clean through the side of the turret.

The Tiger's hatches flew off in trails of sparks. One lone crew man climbed out, and stood for a moment on top of the turret, as the flames spread over the panzer around him. Then the whole machine erupted in a flash of gasoline flames, and sent out a ragged starburst of detonating ammunition and fuel.

Behind it, a dark mass of German infantry began to pour across the Autobahn – so many that the SU destroyer could only stand and fire at the living column. Infantry moved towards the monster, those men remaining brave enough to take on a Red panzer, determined perhaps to destroy this one by bombs or Panzerfausts.

'Herr Feldwebel! In front of us.'

I had been negligent: in my drugged state, I had been mesmerised by the sight of the doomed King Tiger that I had taken my eyes away from the Autobahn to the South. In the gathering dusk, but lit by the parachute flare drifting west, a number of machines were advancing on us along the dead straight asphalt road. These were T34s, I was sure, with the sloped front plates and bulbous turrets of the 85mm gun type. They were about one kilometre from us, but starkly outlined as the flare dropped to earth behind them, showing up their exhaust fumes. To make up for my error, I was determined to be the first to knock one out – but I also saw the two Hetzers in front of me twitch from side to side as their drivers lined up the turretless machines with the track differential, to align and aim their short 75mm guns at the enemy.

I glanced at our ammunition rack below the turret: it held barely a dozen rounds of armour-piercing in all, and half a dozen high explosive. Plus one round in the breech, and one in the loader's brawny hands. I told the gunner to fire when he was sure of a strike.

The Russian panzers fired first, while still moving, and we took an impact on our front plate which rang through the hull with a deafening echo. Another round went straight past us, towards the mass of infantry behind who were breaking out across the Autobahn, and a third slammed into one of the empty SS Hanomags, splitting open the half-track and sending it spinning over on its roof, trailing flames.

My gunner fired, and the tracer flew directly onto the leading Red panzer. There was a puff of debris on its turret front, and then the whole machine, travelling at perhaps thirty kph, span around on its axis, with flames shooting from its hull hatches. With its ammunition exploding, it reared up and ploughed off the Autobahn, crashing into a culvert and shuddering with explosions. Behind it, though, a whole pack of T34s were taking its place, the lead ones firing as they raced towards us, and the ones behind – I could just make out as the parachute flare died away – loaded with infantry holding on behind the turrets.

I shouted orders to my gunner. With such a pack of armour coming directly towards us, we were a stable firing platform shooting at targets which were getting constantly closer and larger, rather than moving laterally. The T34s perceived us through their sights in the same way – but their rolling motion, even over the flat surface of the Autobahn, impaired their firing accuracy. They were obviously well stocked with ammunition, though, and kept firing as they advanced, each shot causing a slipstream of smoke through which the panzers charged on us.

They had not seen the Hetzers beside the road, I realised – and in a second, our two small destroyer machines opened fire with their 75mm guns. The range was less than five hundred metres, and their combined shots blew the tracks off one T34, causing it to veer sideways and collide with its comrade. That second Red panzer was carrying a squad of troops on its rear, and I saw the soldiers being thrown off by the impact, tumbling onto the asphalt, while the T34s that followed simply drove over their bodies without slowing or swerving.

The tiny size of the Hetzer was its greatest strength: low and compact, difficult to see in the dusk, but with enough punch to halt a T34 in its tracks. The Red panzers began to fire high-explosive at the points where the Hetzers were concealed, trying to flush them out. As they did so, they slowed down to steady their aim.

Inside the Panther turret, seconds passed in a fog of explosive fumes and sweat, breathing and cursing, as my gunner laid his aim. Then the turret reverberated with the shot, and the shell case clunked into the collection box even as our round travelled straight into the driver's visor of a leading Russian panzer. I had been a driver myself, and I knew the damage that would cause: the decapitated hull man, the red-hot fragments smashing around the interior, slicing and setting fire to whatever it hit. That T34 slowed suddenly, its rear deck rising up into the air and then crashing down as the panzers behind it steered around the wreck. They closed up in front of it, and we had to fire again.

We wasted a valuable round which bounced off a T34 turret and smashed into another T34 which was carrying infantry. These troops were knocked off the tank as the deflecting shell cut through them – and again the panzers behind ran straight over the men as they fell onto the road. But where they died, it seemed that more Red panzers carrying troops closed the gap; it seemed that even if every last round of ours found its mark, it would never be sufficient to hold back the Red numbers charging against us.

This was the force that we had provoked with our attack on the East: a force with endless resources, endless men, and an endless desire for vengeance. This was what we had created – and this was what would destroy us now; us and the thousands of people swarming across the Autobahn behind us.

We fired again, and took a hit on our turret that smashed onto the gun mantle and made the breech of our 75mm twitch in the impact. I heard the round deflect downward and hit the top of the hull over the hull crew's head. The driver and radio man heard it too, and let out a stream of relieved curses as the shell failed to penetrate the armour above them.

The Red panzers were on top of us then – literally driving into us, and a vicious, confused battle erupted in our sector of the Autobahn, while the Kessel's occupants flooded across the road only a few hundred metres behind us. That was the Reds' objective, clearly: to smash through us and cause havoc among the foot traffic streaming out of the Kessel at last.

My vision in the periscope was filled with the front turret of a T34 that rammed straight into us, trying to bulldoze us aside. The impact made our entire hull recoil, but the Red panzer came off worse, being thrown to one side, its turret and hull pointing away from us. My driver rotated us onto that panzer with the differential, while my gunner was lowering the gun elevation, and we fired at a range of barely ten metres. I saw the shot punch through the back plate of the Soviet panzer, splitting open the armour there so that I could see the engine flashing with fire in its bay. Then the round exited out of the front of the T34 and span away. What carnage had it caused inside – how many broken limbs and ripped bodies? The T34 shuddered once, and went still, starting to burn from the engine.

Chaos was erupting around us.

Someone had fired off red flares, and the lurid crimson light showed up the landscape like a new sunset. The T34s had found the Hetzers in their emplacements, and were intent on destroying them. We fired on one Red panzer as it tried to crush a little Hetzer under its tracks, with the big Russian tread links scrabbling wildly on the Hetzer's roof, ripping off its hatches. Our round went through the exposed lower plate of the Red, and pieces of its hull sides were thrown off as the panzer exploded with the Hetzer still trapped beneath it.

Other T34s had halted to disembark their infantry, and these riders were leaping off, outlined clearly in the red light, and surging past us towards the crossing point in our rear. The Waffen SS men rose from their positions and confronted them – and although I could not hear the shouts over the din inside my Panther, I glimpsed Russian faces contorted with rage at finding the hated SS troops in their way.

I saw a group of SS men firing from behind the remaining Hetzer, calmly operating a MG42 held over one man's shoulder, tearing down the Red infantry line as it charged onward. The Russians were cut to pieces where they ran, but a T34 blew up both the Hetzer and the MG team with repeated rounds of high explosive. The tank destroyer was blown onto its side, crushing the SS men around it, its tracks running at speed as its transmission raced wildly. Blazing gasoline exploded from its rear deck and flooded the ground for many metres.

We were isolated now, with just our Panther and a handful of Panzergrenadiers against the Red mass, against a remaining trio of T34s racing past us in the light of the flares, intent on smashing the Kessel breakout. One Ivan panzer was hit in the side by a Panzerfaust as it rolled forward, which blew open the front hull and caused an explosion that sent the tracks whirling into the scarlet-tinted air. The troops that fired that rocket were immediately crushed under the next Red panzer, which ran them over and sent their bodies shooting out, dismembered, from the rear of its tracks. We hit the second T34 with an armour piercing round as it moved away from us, knocking a great scab of armour from its turret. Inside, I could see through the periscopes the Red crew flailing as their compartment caught fire, the men struggling to climb from the turret but falling back into the flames.

The last T34 span around to face us, opting to finish my Panther before advancing on the crossing site. We fired first, but our round deflected off his front plate and disappeared into the air. His shot on us hit my radio man's gun point in the hull, where the ball-mounted MG34 was located under a curve of armour plate. My radio man screamed, and then went silent – and before we could afford the time to attend to him, we fired on the T34 at a range of twenty metres, putting a round between the gun mantle and the turret ring. The turret jolted, and the gun slumped. The hull hatch opened, and sparks shot out. I could see that the panzer was burning inside, and in a moment two crew men came out of the hatch, one after the other, their uniforms on fire, but armed with a drum-cylinder machine pistol.

My sight of that was obscured by a human face – close up, right against the cupola periscope. It was an Asiatic, Mongolian type face, and in the red light it was twisted into a mask of absolute hatred. Red infantry were climbing onto us, even as we fought their panzers.

I ordered the driver to reverse – and as we lurched backward, I saw the Russian soldier's face disappear as he was thrown off the panzer in the momentum. I caught sight of his tumbling legs as he went, and then a flash as his grenades exploded on the ground. Our engine stalled, and the Panther filled with foul smoke, so thick that we could barely see across the turret. Smoke coiled around the outside too, making external vision through the periscopes impossible. I threw aside the cupola hatch and put my shoulders up into the air.

The Red fighters were all around us, and the SS men were grappling with them, fighting them to the death. I saw an SS man beat down two Red tank crews with an entrenching spade, then seize their machine pistol and turn it on the other Russian infantry. The SS man was blown apart by a grenade, and the Reds swarmed on towards the breakout point.

Below me, in the smoke-filled hull, my driver was trying to restart the engine. There was no sound at all from the radio man.

I saw some of the Red infantry begin to retreat, followed by tracer and grenade flashes. Our men in the crossing point were beating them back, forcing them away from the thousands of people on foot hurrying across the road. One Red soldier was pursued by two civilians, who shot the man down with a shotgun and a rifle, then stood over him and searched his pockets rapidly. Another wounded Russian dragged himself away, unarmed, until a civilian woman chasing after him shot him in the back with a pistol.

All across the ground between us and the exodus over the Autobahn, such scenes were taking place, as the last of this initial Red attacking force was wiped out by the desperate Germans of all classes and arms.

The crossing point had been kept open.

Our engine started, and we rotated the hull again to face the southern Autobahn where I expected more enemy panzers to appear. We opened all the hatches to ventilate the compartment, and then I shouted down for a report on our radio man. There was no answer, so I climbed down under the turret ring and craned my neck through the forward bulkhead to see the situation in the front hull.

On the left, the driver was green-faced, holding his head up to the open hatch and gulping in mouthfuls of outside air. On the right, across the bulkhead, the radio man was sprawled in his seat, with his head thrown back. A piece of the T34's armour-piercing round had entered the compartment through his machine gun port, destroying his gun mounting, and had come to a halt within the radio man's chest. His whole rib cage was torn open, and inside, I realised as I leaned over to see, a fragment of the conical projectile was embedded through his back, into the steel bulkhead behind him.

I opened the hatch above his head, and asked the men to help me remove his body from the panzer.

—

The force that came to relieve us was not impressive. It consisted of a pair of Stugs, one with smoke pouring from its exhausts, a Panzer IV and a single Panther. These were to guard both the North and South borders of the crossing point, together with two 88mm guns towed by half tracks and about one hundred infantry. In a few hours, these units too would join the exodus West and be replaced by units from further back in the pocket – until the entire mass of men, civilians and machines in the Kessel crept westward like a caterpillar, coiling itself up one step at a time, and then uncoiling as it moved.

The mass of people and materiel moving across the Autobahn was colossal. In any minute, several hundred men women and children would emerge from the shadows of the heath, bunch up on the edge of the road, look quickly left and right as if checking for traffic, and then dash across, disappearing off towards the railroad line in the distance. The sparks and glow of exhausts moved among them, as motorcycles, half-tracks and the few remaining cars and trucks made the crossing too.

The Reds did not attack this point immediately with panzers or troops – but they began a bombardment which burst in slow, random patterns across the Autobahn, scattering groups of people or sending vehicles flying end over end. Nobody knew where the next explosion would fall, or whether they would be the next to be hit, or if they would die or be left behind as wounded, like the many injured troops and civilians who were lying in the shadows on the grassland, crying out not to be abandoned.

Our Panther rejoined the Capo's Panther and the solitary Panzer IV. The old Panzer IV was screeching as it moved, and fell behind us slowly as its power began to fail. As we moved away from the road, I looked back, and saw the panzer being swallowed in the ranks of people trudging past it. Where once they would have climbed up on it, begging for a ride, now they seemed to know that the vehicle was crippled, and they ignored it in their trek to the West. The Panzer IV commander, the old panzer training man, came running after us, flagging us down.

'My fuel,' he shouted.

'We have no spare fuel,' I called down. 'I have barely enough for ten kilometres.'

'But I have plenty,' he shouted. 'I have a full tank.'

We began to reverse back to his machine.

The story was an interesting one: his training unit had been equipped with panzers which had been adapted to run on wood-burning carbon monoxide stoves instead of gasoline. But for several months, gasoline had continued to be delivered, and they had amassed a small reserve. We quickly pumped out every drop of fuel from the Panzer IV tanks, and split it between the Capo's Panther and mine. It was not a large amount, but increased our range from ten kilometres to fifty kilometres: enough, in a straight line, to cross the railroad and reach the Elbe.

That was provided that we had no detours, climbed no hills, and made no bursts of speed in combat.

I let the Panzer IV's trainee panzer crew ride on my Panther's front plate, where the angle meant that only able-bodied people can hold on, and we took several walking wounded and civilians onto the hull top and deck. I put the training instructor himself in the empty radioman's compartment, crouching on the shattered seat, with an MP40 and instructions to fire it through the broken gun mounting if needed. He seemed pleased enough with the arrangement. Then we headed west, in the semi-darkness, among the stumbling foot columns and the random explosions of the shells.

My gunner rested his face on the gun sight and went still. I suspected he was asleep, but I thought that he deserved it. I stood up in the cupola, as we swayed over the heathland. I could see no sign of a counterattack by the Reds, although we were on the left flank and the land in that direction was empty and open. That did not make me confident. On the contrary, it was as if the Russians were now allowing us to break out from the Kessel, permitting us to stream out into the western plain. But what choice did we have? The Kessel was a trap, a noose. If this open land was another trap, it had not yet snapped shut.

In the darkness, which was broken only by the flash of explosions and fires, accidents happened. We passed a motorcycle that had been run over by a panzer, the rider and the machine visible for one instant in the light of a shell burst, mangled together in the ground. Any functioning motor vehicle that stopped was set upon and stripped of remaining fuel and ammunition. In this situation, with the scarcity of gasoline, horses were becoming more valuable. From my turret, I saw a pair of Wehrmacht troops descend on a civilian two-horse cart, cut the traces and make off riding the horses, leaving the civilians to continue on foot. A senior Luftwaffe officer whose staff car had broken down threatened the driver of a horse-drawn field kitchen with a pistol, demanding a horse for himself. The officer was quickly disarmed by passing troops, and he began to make his way among the civilians, holding a suitcase.

We passed a few isolated, heathland houses, in some cases with occupants standing in the doorways, watching us mutely. In the light of the flares and burning vehicles along the road, we saw that some of these houses had fresh graves near them, and it was said that these were graves of civilians who had been killed by the Russians as they passed through in the days before.

In the distance, to the front, there were flashes and coils of tracer erupting into the sky, which I believed marked the point where the SS King Tigers were spearheading the movement to the West. As we grew closer, the movement of people faltered and slowed, as the vast bulk of the infantry were unwilling or unable to progress into combat. Many troops simply lay on the ground in the shadows, waiting for others to go forward and take part in the fighting for the advance. Among these were many officers, who stood sullenly, like children, their arms folded, refusing to give orders or to discipline their men. The civilian women mocked and cursed these officers, calling out that *their* menfolk had fought like true Germans. Indeed, it became common to see armed groups of civilian women, wearing helmets and clutching carbines or Russian machine pistols, seeming determined to defend themselves and their children to the last.

Leaving these miserable scenes behind, my Panther approached the head of the column, closer to the sounds of firing and explosions. The Capo's Panther was just in front of me, and following his exhausts, we entered a plateau crossed by ditches and hedgerows which we in the panzers avoided carefully for fear of losing a track.

In the dim light, we halted at a group of panzer crews, standing around a Jagdtiger – one of the massive self-propelled guns built on the King Tiger platform. The huge vehicle, like a bunker on tracks, was immobilised, emitting thick smoke, and men were syphoning off its remaining fuel.

The panzer crews greeted us with blank faces. By this stage, there were no salutes and formalities, and the distinctions of rank were being lost. There was little interest, too, in the differences between the original units or regiments that we had come from: we were all there at that point in time, and we had to combine to maximise our chances of the breakthrough.

'You have two Panthers?' one of them said to us. 'You will be useful. The railroad is ahead, but there's a blockade in front of it. If we can get over the railroad here, we drive straight on to the West. I know definitively that the Twelfth Army is there, after the railroad, waiting for us. We have had messengers coming through, confirming this. But if we wait here, the Reds will simply destroy us at daylight.'

'But why attack the blockade itself?' the Capo asked. 'Why not bypass it?'

'To the North and South are anti-tank ditches and flooded canals. These are things that our forces prepared, to hold back the Russians, and now the Russians are using them. There are Red panzers hidden up and down there too. We could find a way through all that, but it would take hours, and by then the sun will be up. As soon as daylight comes, the Red planes will cut us to pieces. The blockade is not our construction, the Soviets have built it in the past few days. Therefore we believe it is a rushed piece of work, possibly not finished. We must break through it now.'

As we moved up to the front, the Jagdtiger was destroyed with a demolition charge – that massive machine, the equivalent of two Panthers in steel and resources, was simply left burning beside the road.

The forces for attacking the railroad were our two Panthers, a remaining King Tiger, several Stugs and some mobile 20mm Flak panzers which we called the Wirbelwind. These remarkable machines were quadruple 20mm cannon in open turrets on a Panzer IV chassis, suitable for strafing ground targets as well as anti-aircraft fire. Their presence gave me confidence, but the sight of the infantry that was to accompany us was worrying.

We had several dozen Fallschirmjager, the elite forces that we could trust to give their all. But they were supplemented with Volkssturm men and boys: the under sixteens and over fifties, armed with Panzerfausts and carbines, completely untrained. There were several civilian police units too, and groups of panzer troops with no vehicles, artillery men and Flak gunners who had abandoned their guns in the breakout. Regular Wehrmacht troops were there, and a Pioneer officer brought in another fifty or so from the column at gunpoint, ordering them to fight or face instant execution. This officer was backed up by a roaming gang – that is the word that came to my mind – of Kettenhund men, SS men and Pioneer troops, vicious-looking marauders who radiated a desperation to elude the Russian trap.

Forcing the press-ganged troops forward to join the others, they dragged out one unwilling soldier – a lad of eighteen or so – and executed him with a shot in the head. The others moved into the front line with grim faces.

Dawn would come within an hour – and with it the Red bomber planes and the revelation of the extent of the great column behind us. The officers told me that there were ten or twenty thousand people bunched up here, waiting to cross the railroad to get to the West. Perhaps a quarter of them were civilians or walking wounded. Daylight, surely, would bring a level of destruction on a scale that so far we had not witnessed even in the Kessel.

There was no time for preparation or planning. With the aim of breaching the blockade that guarded the railroad, the single SS King Tiger lurched forward into the dark, with our Panthers following in an arrowhead formation, the Stugs beside us and the two Wirbelwind Flakpanzers following among the mix of infantry behind us.

The railroad was on an embankment on the skyline, lit by the flames of burning vehicles. I could see its wide, straight line running left and right, and at its foot we had been told that the improvised blockade position consisted of bulldozed earth, logs and sandbags. The greatest danger would come when we breasted the railroad itself: as we rose up over the railroad tracks, our lower hulls would be exposed to whatever was beyond for a few seconds – and an alert Russian PAK gunner could put a round through our forward transmission from below.

Above the railroad line, the sky appeared to be tinted grey. Was dawn coming so early? The light suddenly brightened, and a long, intense beam shot up into the sky. Inside my Panther, even in the heat and fumes, we all laughed at the sight of that beam. The Russians had switched on an anti-aircraft searchlight!

'My God, that will protect them from the mighty Luftwaffe,' the loader muttered, peering at the sight through his periscope.

'When was the last time you saw the Luftwaffe?' the panzer trainer called up from the hull. 'Was it Christmas, or before?'

It seemed incredible that, with their domination of the sky, the Reds would bother with an aerial searchlight. But then another beam joined the first, and then a third – and I could see that these were extremely powerful lights, sending long shafts of brilliant white light up into the smoky air above the railroad. The enemy strongpoint was still wrapped in shadows below it. As we closed to five hundred metres, and there was no reaction from the blockade, the searchlight beams quivered, moved through the air – and then descended directly on to our panzers.

Our laughter turned in a moment to shouts of pain and alarm. The lights were dazzling, brighter than any light I had seen before, surely more powerful than any normal anti-aircraft beam. They transformed the space in front of us into a wall of blinding fog, in which it was impossible to make out any perspective or dimensions. My driver slowed, and I used the magnetic compass to keep him driving straight ahead, hoping that the other vehicles would do likewise. Fear gripped my stomach and made my hands shake uncontrollably; we were lit up like showground targets, blind and lost. Over the din of our engine, I heard another vehicle move close to us, collide with our flank and then move off. Then the rapid, chattering fire of 20mm cannons told me that the Wirbelwind had moved in front, and was shooting up at the searchlights.

We entered a situation of complete anarchy and destruction, even by the standards of combat that I had seen in the East. We were hit by a PAK round on our front plate, causing our transmission to shriek. At the same time, the blinding wall of light was cut in half, and I could dimly see flashes to our right as the Wirbelwind blasted its cannon along the railroad embankment. My vision was impaired by the light, and my retina held brilliant shapes that prevented me focussing properly. My gunner cursed and shouted that he had the same problem – he could not focus on the gun sight. This was a new form of weapon from the Reds: a light so blinding that it prevented men from using their weapons.

I ordered our driver to steer us to the right, out of the blinding light, into the area of darkness that the Wirbelwind had created. We were hit again by PAK rounds, two slamming into our turret and blowing the periscope glass down onto me. I could now only see to the front, and there I thought I could make out a wrecked searchlight up on the embankment, and two more lights sweeping their beams randomly onto our forces. Machine gun and PAK fire was coming from the blockade point, only a few hundred metres away. I saw the Wirbelwind's quadruple 20mm cannon tear a row of explosions along the top of the embankment, and then another one of the searchlights exploded in brilliant pieces, and went dark.

The remaining light continued operating, moving up and down the embankment and sweeping its blinding beam over our forces. We almost collided with the SS King Tiger, which was firing with a lowered gun onto the blockade, advancing a few metres between each shot. Unable to see anything else, I ventured my head up out of the cupola.

The battle for the railroad was erupting in fits and starts, as our men and machines threw themselves at the resistance points, cut down by the enemy guns and dazzled by the powerful light. Two Stugs had been destroyed, and their crews were clambering out, shielding their eyes against the light. These men were picked off one by one as they tried to jump clear, by machine guns firing from the blockade. One Stug exploded in flames, sending its tracks and wheels arching through the air for many metres. Our two Wirbelwinds were firing defiantly up onto the railroad line, where the remaining searchlight was flashing its blinding cone back and forth over us. Among all this, our infantry were charging the Soviet blockade, running into the light and explosions in ragged groups.

I gave instructions to my gunner, and aimed our gun roughly at the blockade, and fired our remaining high-explosive rounds into the sandbags and earthen walls. The timber and earth blew up, lifting the Red occupants into the air in a jumble of bodies and debris. A PAK gun fired on us, the tracer deflecting off the front plate just a few metres below me, but then the Capo's Panther charged past us, firing at zero range, until he rammed the blockade itself with his bow. His Panther's tracks clawed madly at the mounds of earth, but sank into the debris that our shells had created, becoming stranded. Beside him, the King Tiger moved along the blockade, firing with his lowered gun into each aperture.

I ordered my driver to ram the blockade, and we lurched onto the position, as Red machine gunners shot at us from either side, with their bullets smacking off our armoured hull. My driver used the differential expertly, to rotate the panzer and crush the dug-in positions – and then, on my order, we began to mount the embankment beyond the blockade.

That last high-powered searchlight began to turn onto us, and I saw that this was a device mounted on a T34 chassis, with a huge projection disc bigger than any searchlight I had seen, even in the Reich. We reached the ridge of the embankment and rammed the machine before it turned its beam fully onto us, knocking it sideways. The T34 hull span off down the slope on the other side of the ridge, with the powerful beam now directed west towards the Red lines. Perhaps this saved us, because a storm of tracer rounds flew up at us from the land beyond, but all the shots went wide. The searchlight panzer caught fire, and began to burn, as its massive lens burst open and the light died. My Panther gripped the stones of the railroad line itself, and I felt the thump of each railroad girder as we passed over the top – and then we crashed down onto the obverse slope, where we knew nothing about the forces ranged against us.

We ploughed to a halt on a slope of loose stones. My cupola periscopes were cracked and dusty, making forward vision difficult. When I was sure that we were below the skyline, so that I was less of a target for snipers, I went up through the cupola to see what was in front of us.

Dawn was close – that much was evident. Not the false, blinding dawn of the power searchlights, but a blue mark across the sky. Below us, Red infantry were retreating, running from us over the

earthworks which we Germans had built to defend the zone. In
the distance, as the land fell away to the East, I saw a corridor of
flames and explosions which surely marked the limit of the Twelfth
Army's advance. If we could make it to that corridor, we would have
a chance of making it onward to the Elbe.

The dawn light rose, as the remaining vehicles and infantry of
our assault group reared up over the railroad lines and slithered
down the slope. None of the Stugs had survived; one Wirbelwind
was intact, and another joined us as a chassis tractor with its open
turret blasted away. The SS King Tiger laboured over the ridge in
the grey light, with flames licking around its engine bay. The huge
machine shuddered and ground to a halt, its tracks sinking into the
loose stones, as its crew extinguished the flames.

The infantry had survived at a rate of perhaps forty percent or
less. The Fallschirmjager came in ones and twos over the railroad,
shouldering their guns and with their faces set under masks of dust.
The Volkssturm people came supporting each other, trailing their
Panzerfausts behind them, boys carrying the old men and vice versa.
The Wehrmacht troops came over with their Kettenhund gang
behind them, the soldiers reduced to a platoon and their escorts
down to two men. With this ragged bunch of men and machines,
we had crossed the last barrier that remained before the Elbe and
our salvation.

But what of the Capo?

Despite the urgency, I ran back over the railroad to look for
him.

The Capo's Panther was stuck fast on the Eastern side of the
ridge, its tracks ripped off and its transmission burned out. In five
minutes, we had drained its fuel and ammunition, and added them
to my Panther, and then we blew the Panther up with a demolition charge. I looked back to see the engine blown out through
the grilles. Around it, a great mass of people was already starting
to make its way West: the thousands of foot soldiers, stragglers and
civilians that had emerged from the Kessel overnight. I installed the

Capo and his crew on my Panther, and we followed the single King Tiger as it spearheaded the way to the West.

Behind us, the sprawling column followed at a running pace: horses, carts, men and women on foot, and numerous motorcycles, a few cars and Hanomags. I could not count the people, but I guessed at four or five thousand that I could see, with many more evidently still behind them. For many of these people, though, their journey was about to end.

As the dawn broke, the sky behind us, to the East, erupted in red – not the red of sunrise, but the orange and black explosions of Katyusha incendiary rockets. The explosions were tearing across the mass of people advancing over the railroad, sending men, women and children flying through the air in flames, throwing horses, wagons and vehicles end-over-end in spouts of fire. The people close to the railroad began to run like demons, the wounded dragging themselves, soldiers throwing away their guns, civilians becoming trampled in the mob.

The breakout was being sealed by the bombardment, with a line of pure fire that prevented any further Germans coming West. Before I turned away, I saw a single horse charge through the wall of flames, streaming fire, his rider dead in the saddle. Nothing else came through that curtain of death, except pieces of debris and burning liquid.

Those few thousand of us that had crossed the railroad quickly accelerated, fleeing the incendiary bombardment, knowing that each moment made it more likely that we would be caught in the firestorm like those we left behind.

—

Reaching the Elbe

Our column of a few thousand now moved through a landscape seemingly untouched by the war. There was no road, so our panzers moved slowly between copses of oaks and orchards of apple and pear trees, hiding as best we could in each area of cover before dashing on to the next. The foot traffic followed us, but the human column was thinning out as people gave up in exhaustion or from their wounds, and lay down to accept their destiny.

In the occasional house that we found, the civilian occupants urged our troops to enter and remove their uniforms, and to put on the work clothes of absent menfolk. Some of our troops accepted the offer, and disappeared into the houses. There was little attempt to stop them; we all knew that each person now had to face the end of the war as he or she best could. Small fires appeared in the yards of the houses, where uniforms and insignia were burned. Many of these houses took in women and children, who were too tired or fearful to continue, and many civilians left our column in this way.

And yet, as the day continued, the sky overhead remained clear of Soviet aircraft, and the sound of the terrible explosions behind us did not come any closer to us. Again, as our Panther creaked and rattled behind the King Tiger in the lead, I had the feeling that the Reds, for their own reasons, were allowing us to advance towards the Twelfth Army and then the Elbe.

Our group was so small that we could see our flanks in the fields on either side, the left and right of each column being guarded by the most able-bodied infantry, mostly the Fallschirmjager or SS men. At times, they shouted a warning, and Russian armoured cars appeared in the distance. The Red vehicles did not fire on us, and this added to our confusion. The rumour went through the column that the war must be officially over, and that we had missed the momentous announcement. Why else would the Reds stand and observe us without shooting? As the kilometres passed, we became sure that this was the case: that the Reds were now under orders not to fire on us, and our hearts lifted at the thought. We estimated that we had perhaps ten kilometres further to travel before we reached the Twelfth Army's positions, and the corridor that would lead us to the Americans on the Elbe.

As we left the cover of a beech wood, we rounded a copse of trees to find a group of German soldiers standing in front of the King Tiger.

'German troops,' my gunner said, with a yell of excitement. 'We've made it. We are through to the Twelfth.'

I put a hand on my MP40, remembering the Seydlitz men that had tricked our people at Halbe. Beside me, the Capo, standing beside the turret, had his pistol ready, and he gave me an order in a low voice to proceed carefully. The Panther ground to a halt beside the King Tiger, and we studied the German troops in front of us.

They were grimy, unshaven and their uniforms were ragged. They looked hungry and scared. In answer to our challenge, they said that they were Panzergrenadiers of the Twelfth Army, and their insignia matched this - unlike the Seydlitz brigades who wore no emblems. They said that the road ahead was mined, and they had been sent to guide any breakout groups through the fields.

'In five kilometres you will be in the corridor,' their Feldwebel called up to us. 'Many people are passing through there to reach the Americans.'

'Is the war over?' we called down.

'No, but the Reds are going slow today. They had their May Day celebrations last night. They know they have won the war. Lots of Red vodka and ladies for them. See there!'

Two Russian soldiers were asleep under a bush beside the road, surrounded by empty bottles. The German troops had taken their machine pistols as souvenirs.

Of course – it was the day after the great Red Communist festival, May the First, or May Day. It sounded plausible that the Reds would be hungover on this morning, and with the war so close to ending, perhaps they would be less inclined to pursue us.

'We should make the most of this,' the King Tiger commander called to me. 'Before the Reds sober up.'

We took these Twelfth Army German troops up onto our panzers among the wounded, and we followed their directions. It was mid-morning by now, clear and warm, and the unscarred landscape was full of meadows, orchards and timbered houses. The foot traffic followed behind us, a ragged column stretching for several hundred metres in the bright sunlight, men shouldering their weapons, supporting each other and stumbling in exhaustion; other men with no guns, walking in a daze, civilians stooping to drink from animal troughs by the gates between the fields.

The Twelfth Army soldiers guided us down into a road that ran in a cutting between two higher fields on either side: a sunken road with walls of chalk growing with ferns and wild roses. The scent of these flowers was noticeable even over the stink of the panzer and our bodies. It was a scent that suggested to my exhausted mind that we were finally going home. We halted at the command of the guides, who then jumped off and went ahead on foot to reconnoitre.

'We'll check for Reds and come back to you,' they shouted.

We waited, with the engines cut out to save fuel; the King Tiger in front, and my Panther behind. The was the contraction of the engines, the moaning of the wounded, the singing of birds and the tramping of feet coming to a halt as the walking column behind us caught up and halted too. The Capo, standing on my rear deck and leaning on the turret, wiped his face on his sleeve and muttered a prayer that our journey was over.

A few minutes later, a person appeared on the edge of the sunken road. He was an officer, his hands on his hips and his pistol holstered.

He was Russian.

Our troops raised their guns to aim at him, but we held fire as the Red officer stared down at us. One by one, other Red troops appeared above us on the edges of the cutting: fresh infantry with almond-coloured faces, clean uniforms, guns that looked straight from the factory. Fifty or sixty of them stood there on either side, looking down on us. I don't know if the two 'drunken' soldiers from under the roadside bush were among them, but I suspected that they were. Finally, one of our German Twelfth Army guides appeared beside the officer, and shouted to us,

'Comrades, there is no point in fighting any more. The war is not over yet, but it will be over in days, or hours.'

There were jeers and insults from the panzer crews and the troops in the sunken road. But still nobody fired a shot.

'Listen to me,' the German defector shouted. 'Those people who followed after you from the Kessel, at the railroad crossing point. Remember them? They are all dead. Not one of them is alive this morning. The Russians can do as they please with us these days.'

'And what do they want with us in this column?' the Capo shouted to the German. 'Why have they trapped us here?'

'You must understand,' the defector shouted back. 'Among the Russian officers, there is competitiveness. The war has become a sport for them. They are playing games with the Germans now.'

'What do they want?' I demanded.

'The panzers,' the defector called. 'Give this Red officer your panzers in working order, without damage, and leave all the women here. You panzer crews and infantry can go on ahead on foot, but you must leave your civilians here.'

The commander of the SS King Tiger turned around in his cupola to look at me on my Panther. We did not speak, but his face was set in stone. He turned back and began speaking to his crew in the hull.

'Comrades, give them the panzers,' the defector pleaded. 'They want the vehicles in working condition. They want to send them back to Moscow for their parades and their ceremonies, that is all. They will let your men pass through here in return. Even the SS can pass through. This officer is the only Red who will make you this offer. There are other Red officers around who will kill you for sure. Comrades, the war is lost! Accept this offer.'

The King Tiger started its engine in a sudden roar of fumes, and jerked forward a few metres in an aggressive show, making the Russian troops step away from the edge of the sunken channel. The SS Tiger commander stood tall in his cupola, outlined against the sky. I saw the German defector's mouth moving, his hands out-stretched as he pleaded with us, and then I told my driver to start up too, and the Panther crashed into life in a cloud of oily smoke.

I don't know who fired the first shot, but from then on the sunken road became a place of death for us all – German, Russians, soldiers and civilians. Through my engine smoke, I saw a bullet pass through the German defector's head, exiting from the back of his skull in a cloud of red and white against the blue. The Red officer beside him was shot through the stomach, and doubled up, his face contorted. The Russian troops along the edge of the channel initially stumbled back, perhaps confused by the lack of leadership – but then they clearly decided to perform their duty as their training dictated. They began firing down onto us in the sunken road, raking the panzers and the foot column behind with their machine gun fire.

I heard the Capo grunt in pain, and saw him tumble off the Panther, falling among the people on foot who were beginning to scatter up and down the roadway. The Capo was hit again, repeat-edly, and I knew that there was no hope for him, that he was now one of the many fallen of the Kessel who would surely have no grave or headstone.

One of his crew men leaped down from the Panther and went to the Capo's side. All that could be done was to remove his Iron Cross from around his neck, and this was thrown up to me on the Panther's deck. In all the danger and confusion, it was a point of honour to us that a dead man's Iron Cross medal should not fall into enemy hands, but be returned to the wearer's family.

The King Tiger in front of us lurched forward again, its tracks demolishing the rose-covered walls of the channel, causing a landslide that brought several Red troops tumbling down under our treads. I remained up on the turret roof, and, with the Capo's Iron Cross in my hand, I shot at the Red soldiers with my MP40, even as the Panther crunched forward over the landslide and juddered after the King Tiger, aiming for the higher ground where this sunken road came up into the meadows.

Grenades exploded on the rear of the King Tiger, the shrapnel streaming back at my panzer, and I saw the rear deck of the Tiger burn with flame for a moment. That huge, seventy-tonne vehicle leaped up out of the sunken track, its whole front end losing contact with the ground, and then slammed down in the pastures beyond. I saw the commander in his cupola shot through with Russian bullets, his body jerking as he was hit. The King Tiger rolled straight on at twenty kph, straight ahead, aiming West, with flames streaming from its engines. Then my Panther too was up on the grassland beside that panzer, and we ploughed forward, side by side, until I told my driver to rotate back and return to the land beside the sunken road.

We drove back in a cloud of dust to find the Red troops firing down into the path. They were firing off entire magazines, and then reloading and firing again. In my hull, the panzer training man opened up with his MP40, and in the turret we depressed the gun elevation and fired off our remaining coaxial MG bullets at the Red troops. We cut them down in a long scything motion, throwing them off one side of the channel and then the other side. I jumped down from the Panther with my MP40 and ran to the edge of the sunken road, and looked in.

The foot column was decimated in there. Infantry, wounded, civilians and horses were jumbled up in heaps of kicking limbs. The able-bodied were emerging from that carnage, and running towards my Panther, dragging a few civilians and walking wounded with them. In this way, perhaps a hundred people came out of that sunken track, and fell in behind the Panther as it turned and moved out onto the plain. Walking with them behind the Panther, I urged them on – men, women and children, shouting at them to speed up as best they could while we stumbled and tripped after the Panther as it rattled across the meadow to the west. I could see a copse of trees beyond the meadow, with good, dark foliage that might shield us, and I knew that my Panther crew would head for that immediately.

The King Tiger, however, was still careering away from us over the pasture, with flames pouring around the back of its deck.

Overhead, there was the scream of aero engines, and the stark profiles of Sturmoviks stood against the glare. Three of them were swooping on us, cannon beginning to bark over the noise of the Panther engine. We who were running on foot threw ourselves flat on the sweet grass – and saw the Red planes pass overhead, one after the other, the three aircraft all aiming for the King Tiger.

I do not believe that the Tiger's crew intended to save us, or meant to draw the Russian fire by driving out into the open pasture, trailing smoke. I think it was a matter of those seventy tonnes travelling at speed, on a downward slope, perhaps with a transmission jammed in gear while the crew compartment filled with fumes. Whatever the cause, the massive King Tiger charged away from us, out on its own, with the body of the commander slumped on the turret, and fire flickering around its back plate. The Sturmoviks shot the panzer up with ruthless accuracy, piercing the engine deck and turret roof with their shells. I saw the engine grilles fly off in pieces, and large scabs of metal from the turret spin off from the sides. As my column hurried into the comparative safety of the trees, the Jabos turned around and came back for another run. The King Tiger was still moving, leaving a trail of flames and smoke behind it. The cannon shells tore one track off, making the whole vehicle rear up on one side and then slam down, shedding wheels and track links. Still rolling, the hull erupted in a puff of flames, until only the colossal gun barrel was visible, emerging from the fireball. Of the crew, there was no sign whatever.

We, the survivors of the entire column, now only a hundred infantry and civilians plus my creaking Panther, pushed deeper into the pine woods, still heading West.

—

The pine forest was man-made, and laid out on a geometric pattern with firebreaks and access roads at regular intervals. Apart from these open firebreaks, which were narrow, the pine trees screened us overhead, although we heard the noise of planes passing over very low at times.

The first thing that we encountered, in the first firebreak, were the bodies of the same Twelfth Army German infantrymen who had led us into the sunken road. They were lying face down, and had all been executed with shots in the back. Stepping over their bodies, I climbed back onto the Panther to take command of the vehicle for this final stage of the breakout.

The panzer was in a hopeless state. The left and right tracks were on different tensions, making the vehicle veer to one side, and the engine grilles gave out a constant acrid smoke. I could hear the transmission front drive whining in the hull, and I guessed that it might last another ten or twenty kilometres. Driving down the narrow but evenly surfaced road between the fir trees improved our fuel use, but it also meant that we could not traverse the turret more than a few degrees, as our gun barrel was obstructed by the trees. Only in the junctions between the road and the firebreak channels which ran left and right at intervals of about one thousand metres could we turn our gun to the side – and we soon found that these junctions were to be feared.

As we approached the first one, our infantry reconnoitred ahead and gestured to us that the way was clear. We moved the Panther forward to the gap, then surged across the few metres of exposure where the firebreak extended into the distance on either side. We paused between the trees beyond, to let the foot traffic make the crossing too. The first dozen troops and civilians hurried across, keeping their heads low. As a second group stepped out, shots came from the firebreak to the left, and a civilian man tumbled onto his front and went still. Another shot felled a Fallschirmjager who was helping a wounded woman to cross, and the bullet seemed to pass through him and hit the woman also. She lay, squirming on top of the paratrooper's dead body, until she also was hit by the sniper, her head emitting a cloud of blood before she went limp.

I could see no sign of the sniper, no smoke or movements. I had the Panther reverse across the open space to form a barrier, and the people surged across in its cover. From inside the turret, I heard bullets smacking off our armour plate, and I feared that the Reds would use an anti-tank rifle or rocket launcher on us. We traversed the turret and fired a precious high-explosive round into the trees, which went zig-zagging from one tree trunk to another before exploding further down the firebreak. When I saw that the last of the people had crossed, I moved the Panther forward.

In this way, we crossed three firebreaks, each time losing a handful of people to snipers on the left or right, but each time bringing with us the bulk of the column. At one point, the Reds tried to mortar us, but their rounds deflected off the trees before they fell, and burst in the air some distance away. Some of our troops were wounded by this shrapnel, and we had to leave them where they fell, still clutching their guns. At the next firebreak, we cut the Panther's engine entirely, and in the sudden silence I heard shots from behind us, where the wounded had been left. Whether that was a sniper, or the wounded killing themselves, it was impossible to say.

Finally, we saw the edge of the forest ahead of us: an area of smoke at the end of the forest track, under a clear sky. We did not pause, but accelerated towards it, as we could see Red infantry moving between the trees around us, following our progress. When we broke out of the forest itself, we came onto an area of burned ground, still smouldering, which was strewn with wrecked vehicles and charred bodies. A row of Panzer IVs stood there, blackened with fire, lined up as if on an inspection parade. The corpses of their crews were jammed in the hatches, with ravens perched on their limbs. We steered around this spectacle, believing that the corridor held open by the Twelfth Army was now very close. I estimated that it was one kilometre or so, and on either side we heard sporadic fighting, suggesting that the enemy were pushing into the corridor with every moment that passed.

We aimed towards a gap between low hills, which I believed led to Juterborg, where the Twelfth Army should be. The distance from the burned ground to that gap was barely a kilometre, but the ground was uneven, and the Panther could only proceed at walking pace, with the column stumbling in our wake. We crossed a hundred metres, with the Panther juddering as if it was about to explode, then another hundred, and by now the survivors of our column were breaking into a hobbling, frantic run, drawing on their last reserves of energy and hope to make this final dash.

I saw a group of houses ahead, which I thought might be the outskirts of Juterborg. Artillery began to fall on us: heavy-calibre field guns which lifted great chunks out of the ground and scattered them into dust. These explosions fell to our right, with debris cutting down a few of our people on that side as they ran. Then the Red gunners recalibrated, and the shells fell across our front, making a curtain of explosions that we would have to run through. I dropped down into the turret, hearing the smash of shrapnel and stones against the armour plate. One shell landed close to us – and the pressure wave made the whole Panther flatten and then bounce up as it passed over us. The shockwave moved through the panzer, making blood spurt from my nose and leaving my ears ringing.

I realised that the engine had died, and I could dimly hear the driver trying to start it. I decided that the Panther was probably finished, and told the crew to exit and find shelter before the whole vehicle was turned over by an explosion.

We stumbled out of the panzer, and threw ourselves onto the ground near the houses. Our column was already taking shelter there: the shattered windows and doors revealed huddled groups with their hands over their heads. I glimpsed a group of Soviet infantry too, on the edge of the houses, also seeking cover, caught in the open by their own bombardment.

I saw a house with a basement window at ground level, its shutters hanging open, and I jumped in there. Ducking down into the basement, I found that it was occupied by several small children, girls of six or seven years, and two women. The women had the children huddled to them, and their faces were clenched in fear. The explosions outside made the whole floor lift up, and pieces of masonry were starting to fall from the walls. As bricks fell loose among us, a pair of boots appeared at the foot of the steps, and a man crashed into the refuge, followed by another man. They crouched on the floor, staring at us. They were Russians.

They were young, barely twenty, and they wore thin tunics, backpacks and steel helmets. The red star on their chest pockets glowed bright in the light from the stairs. Each man was holding a cylinder-drum machine pistol.

They looked at me, at the children and women, and then at the flashes of explosions at the top of the stairs. Then they just shrugged, and sat back against the opposite wall, their guns in their hands, not taking their eyes off us.

I could feel the weight of my pistol in my holster. The Reds showed no sign of violence, despite my uniform. One of them grinned at the children and winked, making 'explosion' noises in his throat. A shell-burst outside made dust pour from the ceiling. The children flinched and whimpered. This cheerful Russian reached into his pocket, and showed the children a picture of his family. The children looked at it in silence, then they looked at me expectantly. Keen to reassure them, I fumbled out the photo of the unknown young woman in *my* pocket, and showed it to them. Everybody nodded in approval – the children, the women and the two Russian lads.

Debris was still falling onto us from the explosions.

One of the soldiers took his steel helmet off, reached it out and placed it on the head of one little girl, saying something in Russian. The girl's head was almost concealed by the green steel helmet. The man leaned back, bareheaded. There was a shell-burst directly in the doorway at the top of the stairs, and debris flew down the steps onto us all. I ducked, covering my head, and threw myself in front of the children. I heard shrapnel smashing down the stairs and hitting the walls around us.

I looked up. The bareheaded Russian man had been hit in the forehead. Where his helmet would have protected him, a long piece of shrapnel projected from the wound. He looked dead. His friend was checking his pulse, feeling for signs of life – and then muttering angrily. His eyes burning, he stared at the child with the green helmet – and reached for his gun.

I shot him twice in the chest, then leaned across and shot him again in the head, while the children screamed. The bodies lay there in front of us, while the shelling went on.

When there appeared to be a lull in the bombardment, I told the women to come with me, to leave that place and join our journey to the West. They refused, preferring to stay in their cellar, whatever the outcome. To save them from more trouble than they already faced, I called to my crew men and we pulled the Russian bodies out of the cellar and left them in a crater some distance away from the houses.

The foot column was slowly reassembling from the shattered buildings, with people emerging in ones and twos. After several attempts, my crew started the Panther again, and we formed up our column and then moved on towards the gap in the hills.

The next troops that we saw were German, and they called to us to keep moving, that the Twelfth Army was directly ahead. These troops were guarding an 88mm gun and a pair of Hetzer destroyers which were dug in to guard the hills, so we believed that they were not defectors. We began to find more troops, dug into foxholes or manning gun emplacements, who told us that the Twelfth Army corridor was still open for us.

With the Panther at walking speed, our ragged, bleeding convoy moved into the corridor itself, and we began to move on towards the West. The corridor was barely three kilometres wide, and on each side there were towers of smoke and constant gun fire, as the German Twelfth Army screens there tried to hold off the Soviet pincers that were seeking to crush the safety zone. Red planes raced overhead – but there was a strong Flak cover here, with 20mm Flak wagons using plentiful ammunition. We saw a Sturmovik shot down, with its wings crumpling as it twisted around on fire, and slammed into one of the hills beside us.

The centre of this corridor was full of targets for the Red Jabos: columns of troops that had made it through the encirclements and the pockets to the East, single panzers such as ours, and a few groups of armour, many horses and hand carts for the civilians. The few farmhouses in this region were burning fiercely, many with improvised cemeteries in their yards instead of vegetable gardens and animal paddocks. One yard contained a T34 upside down in a crater, and another had a complete Stuka panzer-buster aircraft just sitting in its grazing meadow, with its canopy hanging open, surrounded by dead cattle with their hooves in the air. Everywhere were foot soldiers or civilians, scavenging as they trudged West, beneath trees whose branches were blackened with incendiary fires.

If some among us had imagined that the Twelfth Army zone would be a place of safety, it became clear that the danger here was still very great.

At one point, the protective screen on our left seemed to give way, and German Twelfth Army infantry began streaming back into the centre zone, in full retreat, adding to the confusion around us.

118

Officers halted them with shots over their heads, and several troops who had thrown their weapons away were shot dead out of hand. Still, the breach in the defences was there, barely a kilometre from us, and the sound of tanks came through between the shell bursts.

From up in the cupola, I saw two of our Stugs emerge from concealment beside the road, and head towards the danger point. The crews of these Stugs were young teenagers, perhaps sixteen years of age, and they must have known that they were going to their deaths. They went with blank faces, their eyes wide with amphetamines and fear.

I traversed my Panther and moved in support of them, and although my vehicle would now only operate in second gear, we travelled a few hundred metres through the trees and scrub between us and the screen of the corridor. We passed a staff car among the bushes, which contained two Wehrmacht Majors, both middle-aged but fit and unwounded, both simply waiting in their fine car for the passage to be secured for them by the sacrifice of the young men. We clipped the car in passing, tearing off a wheel, and we moved to a firing position, from which we could just see the edge of the corridor itself.

The situation out there was desperate. The two Stugs were firing on a phalanx of T34s which were nosing in on a gap in the defences. An 88mm PAK gun was also firing from a bunker, and remnants of our infantry were crouched in slit trenches and craters, clutching Panzerfausts. A group of Volkssturm men, aged in their fifties, marched past us rapidly, Panzerfausts and carbines held ready to help fill the gap. These men were immediately hit by a shell burst, and their bodies were dismembered across the ground. A gang of Hiwis – the Russian collaborators who feared recapture by the Reds more than anything – ran forward and seized the dead men's guns. These Russian defectors threw themselves into the battle with the reckless courage of men whose death sentence was already passed.

My gunner fired on the leading T34, stopping it dead, and two German troops rushed forward with Panzerfausts to finish it. The rockets tore off the front plate of the Red panzer, while the Red crew were still trying to scramble out of the hatches. The T34 began to explode from inside, with main gun ammunition bursting out of the fractured hull in spirals of smoke and sparks.

My Panther was hit by the other T34s, and a shell split the front edge of our turret, so that I could see daylight between the wall and the roof. Another shell hit our front plate and bounced upward in a spray of debris. I told the gunner to fire all our remaining ammunition – and with those few remaining rounds we hit another T34 which was charging on our 88mm position. We knocked the turret right off that panzer, but the hull kept rolling forward, lurching wildly, until it ploughed into the PAK emplacement and crushed the 88mm crew under its tracks.

On my orders, my Panther began to reverse, with nothing by way of fuel or ammunition left to fight with, as the Stugs and their teenage crews fought on, firing again and again at the ranks of T34s rolling in from the fields beyond. From somewhere, two fresh Panthers came to join the defence: vehicles that seemed to be direct from the factory, in perfect paint and equipment fitted to the hulls. As we reversed away and moved back towards the central zone, we saw many of the Hiwi men, finishing their ammunition, stand up and walk towards the T34s, deliberately exposing themselves to the deadly fire. For the Hiwis, it was better to die like that, quickly and anonymously, than spend the rest of their lives in the Gulag, knowing that, because of their collaboration, their families were sharing that fate too.

The two infantry Majors whose car we had just clipped tried to flag us down, demanding a ride, brandishing their pistols. I was not in the frame of mind to suffer these fools, and so I jumped down from the turret and disarmed them. We checked their car, and found two full cans of gasoline in the back. Two full cans! That was enough for another thirty kilometres. The two officers scowled as we filled our tank, then offered us a box of gold watches if we would accept them as passengers. We took two Panzerfausts from some Volkssturm men rushing past us, and armed the two Majors with these, sending them up to the front line with kicks from our hobnail boots. The Volkssturm assured us that the officers would be a valuable resource, worth a whole platoon of Panthers, and began driving them on with their carbines.

The perimeters of the corridor were shrinking every minute. The Red planes circled overhead, weaving between the Flak, firing into the fleeing columns or unloading fragmentation bombs along our route. These bombs separated in the air into smaller containers of explosives, which scattered wildly over a huge area, exploding in torrents of ball bearings and shrapnel.

I thought that I was immune to the sight of death and injury, but the sights we saw on that final few kilometres were astonishing. A civilian bus, commandeered by staff officers, was bogged down in a rut and hit by a fragmentation burst. The thin sides of the bus were ripped open, and the bodies of the officers inside tumbled out onto the road, the wounded lying untended as the passing foot soldiers stepped over them. A group of political prisoners in their striped pyjama uniforms were being employed to pull wagons full of possessions: suitcases, paintings and furniture, under the command of an SS unit. A Red plane shot up the whole procession, sending the paintings in their gilded frames flying through the air, and knocking down the prisoners along with the SS. The prisoners who survived ran or stumbled off into the trees towards the perimeter, some clutching the guns taken from the dead SS men.

A house we passed had two elderly men strung up on nooses from its shutters, with a sign around their necks:

We showed a white flag to the Red monsters.

The white flag itself was draped around the dead men's bodies, swaying in the breeze.

A group of armed civilian women had cornered a Russian infantryman inside the corridor, and were asking the passing troops what to do with the man. He stood, bareheaded and sullen, while his fate was discussed. Nobody was interested in him, and the women simply shot him through the head with a pistol, then climbed onto a passing wagon.

A Red fighter plane was hit by Flak high overhead, and the aircraft smashed nose-down into the trees, turning an ancient oak into a blazing torch as high as a church steeple. The pilot came down on a parachute, and became entangled on branches across the road further on. He hung there, ten metres overhead, trying to free himself, the subject of disinterested glances from those trudging past, until somebody shot him through the body.

Metre by metre, we began to leave this zone, entering an area where there were patches of long, narrow meadows shielded by fir trees. In some of these meadows, German aircraft had tried to land, perhaps escaping from the East and finishing their fuel here. One field had an abandoned Focke-Wulf fighter, simply standing in the grass, its engine cowling steaming in the light. In another field, a Junkers 52 plane had crash-landed on its belly, and a man of General rank was kneeling on the ground nearby, retching into the grass.

A few minutes later, beyond the trees, we saw shapes moving in another one of these lush pastures. I could see a glint of metal through the mist, and there was a smell of gasoline in the area. I dismounted from the Panther and went forward with one of the infantry men to see what was happening in there. I expected to see Red tanks manoeuvring into position, or isolated elements of our armour in hiding, sitting out the surrounding battles. Instead, as we crept forwards between the trees, machine pistols in our hands, we saw a sight that few Germans were ever privileged to see.

Through the mist, as the sun burned off the vapour, the glimpses of pale metal turned to a definite outline, which at first was blurred by the mist, but then became clear. In a few moments, as the metal object moved across the secluded pasture, both I and the infantry-men with me drew breath and lowered our guns.

The object was an aircraft – of a design that we had seen in the newsreels and soldiers' magazines, presented to us as the greatest of its type – but surely none of us ever believed that we would see one in person. This was a Messerschmitt 262, the legendary jet-powered *Schwalbe* or swan, the sleek and beautiful twin-engined creation that was one of our wonder weapons. I was astonished at how big it was – in the newsreels, it seemed so much smaller – and I was astonished too at the crude nature of its construction. Its metal panels were evidently hammered by hand, and their metal skin was unpainted except for the German cross on its fuselage and the swastika on its tail fin.

'No propellers!' one of the foot soldiers said to himself. '*Hier ist wunder!* Here's a miracle!'

The aircraft was balanced on its wheels, which were sinking into the lush turf. It was being dragged by a team of oxen – the simple, wagon-pulling oxen that had been bred in this part of Germany for thousands of years. The oxen were roped together, and the rope was looped around the 262's undercarriage, and metre by metre those ancient beasts, guided by a farm boy of ten years of age, were dragging the jet plane through the grass towards the safety of the trees.

We common soldiers stood mute at this sight. What did this mean for us, and for Germany? Our wonder weapons existed, they were there in front of our eyes, and they were superbly designed with the greatest science that human kind could summon. But the machine was crudely made, it was uneven, and it was being hauled like a medieval cart on its wheels by a gang of oxen, each animal trailing a cloud of flies from its arse. And it was leaking fuel: splashes of liquid were pouring from its hull, making the whole forest reek.

'Don't light a cigarette, my friends, or you're all finished.'

A Luftwaffe pilot squatted beside us, grinning. He was middle-aged, and he looked exhausted, with hollow cheeks and thin hair oiled over a balding skull. His flying boots were perfectly polished, but his moustache was yellow with nicotine. He gave us an account of how he had brought the plane down in an emergency landing on the pasture, leaking the precious jet fuel that was more valuable to the Reich than gold.

'But how shall I get to the West now?' he murmured. 'Everything is lost. Perhaps I shall have a cigarette anyway, when you are safely gone.'

We shook hands with him, eager to clasp the hand of a legend. Our complaints, our bitter jokes about the Luftwaffe were forgotten for a minute, as we watched the superb aircraft being pulled into the shadow of the elm trees, where it was to be stored, the pilot told us, until it could somehow be returned to service. As we left the thicket, the lowing of the oxen began, a sound that I recognised as the beasts of burden being unyoked from their load.

A minute after that, the whole corner of the forest behind us was lit up, and we turned to see a colossal orange fireball climbing into the air above the trees. The fireball was dripping with burning fuel, rolling over as it rose, so hot that it burned the mist from the treetops for hundreds of metres around. The farm boy who had driven the oxen came running after us, shouting hysterically.

'He lit a cigarette, the fool! As if he wanted to die.'

Slowly, these scenes and many others fell behind us, and the sounds of fighting from the perimeter became more distant. Our panzer creaked and rattled at walking pace through a smokescreen, our eyes streaming with tears which we had not shed in the battles, and entered a zone which appeared to be organised in some manner of discipline.

Kettenhund men were directing the traffic onward, and the improvised defences and emplacements gave way to properly constructed ditches and trenches. The troops here were a mixture of the completely fresh and the exhausted, and the equipment likewise was both new and old. A number of immaculate PAK guns, their wheels barely muddy, were manned by gunners who resembled scarecrows, thin and ragged. A unit of Hitler Youth troops, in clean uniforms and recent haircuts, were manning a defence point that consisted of an old Panzer III with no wheels or tracks, standing in a mound of barbed wire. The troops were from a great variety of units and regiments, including armed police and Volkssturm men.

Amazingly, there were field kitchens too, giving a ladleful of hot soup to anyone, soldier or civilian, who passed. I ate my ration on the Panther's rear deck, leaning on the turret, surrounded by wounded men and children. The engine smoke coated us with grime, and the fumes made us nauseous, but we were properly inside the Twelfth Army sector, heading for the Elbe.

As we rolled past a group of soldiers clustered around an armoured car, one of them turned to us and shouted something. I didn't catch it, but some of the children heard, and began to tug my sleeve.

'Feldwebel?'

'What is it, lad?'

'The Fuhrer is dead now.'

We stopped at the next group of troops and listened to their radio set for a few minutes. It announced that the Adolf Hitler had died in the fight for Berlin, only thirty kilometres to the North of us. The war continued all the same, in the hope of a final victory. Some women were weeping, and some of the troops stood around, talking openly of suicide. I felt little – except for the pain in my back wound, for which I took the last of my drugs.

—

The Twelfth Army sector around Brandenburg in front of the Elbe was a landscape of destruction and constant movement. The perimeter was being held by the remnants of the Twelfth and the escaped Ninth Armies, but the whole zone was being pressed heavily by the Reds – except for the Elbe itself on the Western boundary, which faced the silent, unmoving Americans on their bank. Vast columns of vehicles and people were making their way across the rolling countryside towards the river. The Reds controlled the sky despite our Flak, and their Jabos came over frequently, strafing the columns, the buildings and the open land. We knew that if the Russians wanted to, they could bomb the sector into dust. They were holding back, waiting for the end of the war, and perhaps seeking to maximise their catch of humanity. Leaflets cascaded down from the sky, urging everyone in the sector to remain static and stop resisting the advance of the Red Army.

Hitler is dead. Berlin has surrendered. The war
has no logic and it must end now.

In addition, voices spoke to us through loudspeakers amplified at incredibly high volume. These were the voices of Seydlitz officers, and the warm spring breeze carried them for kilometres across the landscape. The words were indistinct, but we caught *Surrender, Peace, Life, Goodwill* and a few others. We listened to this, and the drone of the aircraft overhead, as we joined a massive flood of people heading towards the river.

It was rare now to see armed troops; most had thrown away their weapons, and they walked with hands in their pockets or supporting their backpacks. Most epaulettes and other signs of rank had been removed from their uniforms, and the meadows were scattered with badges, caps and jackboots. Men's civilian clothing was prized now, and many men who wore the trousers and shirt of farm workers had the bearing of recent professional soldiers. Schnapps and other alcohol was in ample supply, and many people were to be seen lying drunk beside the road, desensitised to whatever they had witnessed and whatever fears possessed them.

The fields and roadsides were lined with abandoned vehicles, both mechanised and horse-drawn. There were a few panzers among the trucks, Kubelwagens and cars, but it seemed that most armoured vehicles had been left behind in the Kessel and the other battle zone. Our Panther was the only one of its type that we saw, and it was close to dying under us. At a junction in the roads, a huge crater barred the way to heavy vehicles, and the foot traffic crossed on a wooden bridge. We tried to take the Panther around this obstacle into the meadows, but the fields close to the river were marshy, and the tracks soon sank in deeply.

There was no benefit in trying to make the machine go on any further. The river Elbe was within walking distance, the fuel was gone, and the engine was in danger of catching fire.

We drove the old panzer further into the marshes, knowing this was the end, and not wanting the machine to fall into any other hands, either Russian, American or even German. With the wounded and the civilians lifted off, we drove the Panther in second gear for a few more metres, until it hit a stretch of water surrounded by bulrushes. It began to subside, the engine end going down first. We jumped clear and watched it sink.

With fumes rising into the air, the front plate rose up, the long gun barrel dripping with marsh water. The cupola, from which I had seen so much and given so many orders in the heat of combat, filled up with the stagnant water, and slid below the surface. There were some final bubbles and fumes. I stood there in silence as the green weeds gathered over the Panther, and, when the surface was still, I turned with my crew and we walked at the head of our small column along the choked roads down to the great River Elbe.

The approaches to the river were packed with people of all types: civilians, unarmed troops, and some combat troops who still carried their weapons. Among these were Waffen SS men of the Panzer Corps who were pushing through the crowds ahead of us, forcing the ranks of people out of their path. I could just see the river down at the foot of the slopes, over the heads of the thousands of people trying to make their way down there. The water looked black, and the river was about two hundred metres wide. There was a single bridge at this point spanning the width, the other bridges to north and south having been destroyed in April to prevent the Americans crossing. This bridge was a narrow, wood and steel construction, and as we came onto the slope I saw the reason for the so many people still waiting to cross over: the bridge was blown up in its central point, and only a single file of people could walk across to the American side, one at a time.

The American bank looked largely deserted; there were no panzers or gun emplacements there, and no American infantry that I could see. I spoke to a Leutnant of an artillery unit beside me in the crowd, and he told me that the Americans had pulled their men back several kilometres to the West of the river.

'They don't want a conflict with the Russians,' he said with a shrug. 'But look at all these people. There must be fifty or sixty thousand people here. Will the Amis let all of us cross over to them?'

I squinted down at the opposite bank. The line of people who had already crossed over the damaged bridge were simply fanning out across the grassland on that side, trudging off to the West. There was a huge pile of discarded small arms over there – carbines, rifles and machine guns, helmets and Panzerfausts – indicating that the troops saw no need of them when on the American side. I saw some men trying to swim the river, against the swollen and fast-flowing current. Some emerged on the American bank, but many seemed to disappear under the dark water and not resurface. Someone had tried to make a boat out of a bridging pontoon, but this sank slowly as its crew paddled across, and the men slipped away under the water.

Ahead of us, the SS men were beating a path through the crowds in their rush to reach the riverbank. Shots were fired, and in a minute we stepped over the bodies of two artillery cadets who had evidently sought to argue with the SS. There were other bodies lying neglected on the ground: wounded men and civilians who had succumbed, and those in their final throes who had nobody to assist them. Lost children wandered through the thousands of adults, crying out for their relatives. The civilians in my column gathered up half a dozen of these children, and we remained together as we shuffled slowly forward to the bridge.

On the approaches, there were troops guarding the bridge itself, who sought to extort valuables from those people waiting to cross, in return for jumping forward in the crowds. For a gold watch, a good camera or a diamond ring, you could go directly to the bridge itself without waiting. At first the people cursed these troops, but the sound of a bombardment from behind us, up on the slopes above the river, and the screams of the wounded from those explosions, brought many offers of payment. The crowd was swaying, and people were falling underfoot and being trampled. From somewhere, a horse bolted through the crowd, kicking and trampling anyone who got in its path, until it was felled with shots. When a Red aircraft flew low overhead, not firing but low enough for us to smell the vapour of its exhausts, the crowd panicked and tried to storm the entrance to the bridge itself.

Many people were crushed or trodden to death here, and inevitably it was the frailest and weakest who suffered the most. The banks of the river were steep clay cliffs, and many civilians fell into the water and did not resurface. In all this chaos, the remnants of my column clambered finally onto the bridge, and we began to walk across the planks in single file, with the water twenty metres below us, squeezing past the damaged section in the centre.

Setting foot on the opposite bank was a strange experience.

During everything we had seen and done in our breakout from the Kessel, the thought of the American side of the Elbe had been constantly in our minds. Now that we trod on the grass, without one single American soldier, panzer or American plane in sight, the sensation was unreal, as if my feet were numb. With my crew and the fragments of infantry and civilians still with us, we left our pistols and other weapons on the pile of side arms, a pyramid of gunmetal which rose to a height of four metres. All I kept was the photo in my pocket, and the Capo's Iron Cross on its ribbon, snatched from his body in the sunken road. As we turned to leave, a Kettenhund came staggering towards us.

This man was drunk, and waving a pistol at us. Our civilians shrunk away from him, while he gestured with the pistol at the medal in my hand.

'I'll take that,' he said, with a reek of schnapps.

'You didn't earn it,' I said.

'The American boys pay me ten bucks for an Iron Cross,' he laughed. He used the American word *bucks*, not *dollars*, as if he was now one of them. 'I'll give you two bucks for yours now, so you can get a meal and a shave.'

Just as I hit him in the face, he shot me.

That was the way my war ended, in May 1945, on the West bank of the Elbe, under American occupation but without an American in sight. After my two years of fighting, after Kursk and the retreat to the West, after the Halbe Kessel and the fields full of bodies. After everything I was ashamed of, and everything that I took pride in, my war ended with a drunken Kettenhund shooting a hole in my shoulder blade. As I lay on the West bank of the Elbe, watching the boots of my Panther crew as they kicked the Kettenhund man to death right there and then, I could only close my eyes against the sky and accept that everything that we had done was now at an end.

—

My crew took me to a Red Cross centre in the American zone: an improvised hospital in an abandoned school building on the outskirts of Hanover. My injury was extensive, and added to the existing wound in my back, recovery was slow. I spent days in the grounds of the school building, listening to American radio shows and playing cards. At first, the food that we were given was so rich and sweet that it made me vomit, as my stomach was accustomed to Wehrmacht rations and water. We German men would stand at the table at meal times and shake our heads in wonder at the sight of the hot dogs, scrambled eggs and bread rolls, the biscuits and Hershey bars we could buy from the store. The nurses were Red Cross volunteers and nuns of various countries, who could not be bettered anywhere for the care they gave us.

My uniform was folded in a locker, and I took to wearing old civilian trousers and shirt which came from the hospital clothing bank. I shaved every day, and smoked cigarettes in the sunshine. The patients did not speak to each other about their experiences in the war. Once, I saw a new patient brought in, who had been injured in a knife fight. I thought I recognised him as one of the SS men from the bridge crossing, but I said nothing about this, and neither did he. My Panther crew were dispersed to prisoner processing camps in the American and British sectors, and I heard that the civilians that had been in our column simply disappeared into the landscape of Germany.

I was interrogated by an American sergeant, who wanted only to know if I was a member of the National Socialists. He was less interested in my war record; there were simply so many of us to be processed. May 1945 turned to June, and then July.

Now the wisdom of surrendering to the Americans was confirmed absolutely in my mind, because everybody knew that the information we had about our prisoners in the East was zero, literally zero. The millions of men who had surrendered to the Reds East of the Elbe had melted into the Soviet system, and nothing was known of them. Some people said that they were in the Central Soviet Republics, places that lay beyond the Caucasus Mountains, and now might just as well be on the moon. Other people said that they were in Siberia, or Mongolia, from where (the Hiwis and Red prisoners had always told us) not even Russians can ever return. We in the West felt vindicated in our determination to escape that fate, while many of us also felt uneasy, knowing that luck had played a large part in our diet of hot dogs and chocolate.

At the same time, the future of the Western part of Germany was becoming clearer. The Western Allies were investing in rebuilding the cities they had destroyed. Anything could be bought for a price: coffee, cosmetics, guns, gasoline, morphine, colour magazines, cameras, bourbon. I was offered a Jeep if I could scrape together ten Iron Crosses plus Luger pistols to go with them.

'They gotta be Lugers,' my American contact insisted. 'Walthers won't do it.'

The streets were full of German girls walking with American GIs, and glum German boys watching them pass. The atmosphere in the streets, strangely, felt like some time before the war, when the future seemed full of possibilities. My future, though, was uncertain. My only remaining family had been the Wehrmacht, and I had no home, no occupation and no resources. At night, the hospital ward was full of weeping and cries, as the men dreamed of their battles.

Some nights, I did not let myself sleep, knowing I would see the Halbe Kessel again, and above all the dead Russian man in the cellar, whose friend gave his steel helmet to the German child. Why did that one Russian visit me at night, after all the scores that I had killed, the thousands that I had seen killed? Because I showed him the photo of the girl in my pocket – was that why? I lay on the bed, in my own personal Kessel of the mind, wondering about all this.

I knew the time was approaching for me to leave the hospital. One by one, the wounded German men that were in the hospital were able to leave, and most were discharged into the civilian population. The nurses saw that I was troubled by this, and they didn't understand why.

'But you have your sister,' one nurse said to me after changing the dressing over my shoulder wound for the last time, as we watched humid rain on the windows of the ward, late one afternoon. 'Or is she actually your girlfriend? The photo that you keep.'

I didn't answer.

'What is her name, Wolfgang? You have never told us her name.'

The photo was in a frame on my locker. I made the frame myself from pieces of a medical box, and fitted a glass over it from a piece that I found in the gardens. I looked at that photo each day, remembering the girl's mother and the way that she died on the rear deck of my Panther in the Kessel.

To be frank, I had started to imagine a new life with that girl, and the remnants of whatever family she had – to replace the complete absence of family in *my* life outside the panzer troops. If I must be honest, I had spent my time in the hospital imagining my future life with that girl, and a house that we might have in the American sector, and me finding a paying job, maybe working with machines. Any solitary man knows the kind of thoughts that I had.

'What is her name, Wolfgang?'

I had no idea of her name. But there was an address on the back of the photo, in a town not far from the Elbe, and the more I thought about that girl, the more I thought that I should go and visit her. And so it was, at the beginning of August 1945, that I left the hospital in a civilian suit and tie, with a backpack and a small bunch of flowers that the nurses made for me, because they knew where I was going and why.

I found a lift on a postal truck, and then a farm cart – both driven by men my age who must surely have been in the war. We didn't ask each other for details, watching the streets full of people at work, clearing the mounds of rubble and putting their homes back together for the future. People stood in lines, passing bricks from hand to hand, while American bulldozers cleared whole blocks and American trucks brought in whole loads of timber and concrete to build everything again.

Had the Americans forgiven us, then? It seemed that they had, and it felt to me that the Halbe Kessel was now in the distant past, and that its secrets would be locked for all time in the forests East of the Elbe, and in the minds of those who had witnessed those events. America was our future now – America, where anything could be forgiven, forgotten and lost. As the cart halted outside the address, I felt that this was *my* future too, this new world of building and forgetting the past.

The house was shuttered, and the doors were locked.

My heart was pounding with apprehension, as it used to do before combat. Getting no answer from the silent house, I asked a neighbour if they knew of the girl, showing the photo in its frame. The old lady took me into her own house next door, and sat me at a table in a darkened kitchen.

'Is she still living there?' I asked. 'Where is she?'

The neighbour woman wrung a cloth in her hands.

'The Americans have been very good to us,' she said.

'Yes, yes. I see that. But this young lady?'

'The Americans have been generous, and have restored order. We are very lucky here, compared to those in the East under the Reds. What the women have suffered over there, it is indescribable.'

'Yes, we are lucky. I myself made great efforts to reach the West, to escape the Reds,' I told her. 'Now I see that the journey was worthwhile. But this girl, where is she?'

'We have no complaints against the Americans, young man. It is to be expected that in any army there will be one or two bad apples, a small number of problem soldiers. I am sorry, young man, but the girl in your photo is no longer with us.'

'She has left?'

'She is dead. It is very regrettable. In any army, there will be one or two who do not obey the law. We are lucky that the Americans have so few of these, compared to the Russians. You must not be angry, and you must not look for revenge, please. The fact is that the young lady was killed by an American soldier some weeks ago. If you must know the details, he was drunk and forced himself on her, and then he strangled her. But the law has been applied, you see. The man himself is in their military prison, and it is said that he will hang for the crime. Our mayor is very close to the Americans, and he says that the man will surely be hanged. But such events are rare, they are almost unheard of in the American sector, as you can imagine. We must all try to forget this event now, because it is not good to remember these things for long.'

I nodded, in the darkened kitchen, listening to the sounds of the reconstruction outside.

I walked away from the house in the sunset, through the summer fields, not knowing where I was going next. In these meadows, there were junkyards of armoured vehicles, where long rows of our panzers were lined up in the grass: rusting, abandoned and silent. The little Hetzers, the Stugs, the great Tigers, the great Panthers; all waiting in the sunset, empty, row upon row, leaking oil, with birds making nests in their turrets. It seems that when a war ends, there is too much metal left over, too much steel, and all the panzers lose their value.

Truly, the neighbour lady was correct.

It is not good to remember these things for long.

—

For more reading about WW2 panzer combat, we
highly recommend the classic…

'Tiger Tracks' by Wolfgang Faust

Written in the late 1940s by a veteran of the Wehrmacht
Heavy Panzer Battalions, 'Tiger Tracks' was his brutal portrait
of the Russian Front's mesmerising violence and cruelty.

*"Among the most impressive narratives of the Eastern Front that
I have read. The pages are alive with characters - their machines,
their struggles, their decisions and their pain. Readers will finish
the book haunted and truly moved, the mark of a great story."*

- Chris Ziedler, translator of **'The Last Panther.'**

Made in the USA
Monee, IL
02 April 2021

64372568R00079